SPELLING
self-taught

A
TEACHING-MACHINE
BOOK

By **LESTER D. BASCH**, M.A. and
MILTON FINKELSTEIN, Ed. D.

1975 EDITION

Published by
Melvin Powers
WILSHIRE BOOK COMPANY
12015 Sherman Road
No. Hollywood, California 91605
Telephone: (213) 875-1711

Printed by

HAL LEIGHTON PRINTING CO.

P. O. Box 1231
Beverly Hills, California 90213

Second Printing, 1963

CONTENTS

INTRODUCTION

Spelling Self-Taught may be one of the most important books you have ever read. This book, which is itself a teaching machine, can help you to improve your spelling—to set you on the road to that correctness which marks the well-educated person. Your ability to spell is a continuing advertisement of your opinion of yourself. There is no reason why any person who wants to spell well should not be able to do so, for spelling is a skill which can and should be learned by all. With this up-to-date teaching machine book as your guide, you will be able to master spelling in just a few months.

Here are only a few situations in which the inability to spell is a serious handicap.

—Students in schools and colleges do less well than they should because errors in spelling mar work which is otherwise well done.

—Adults who otherwise have the ability to gain promotion in their jobs are held back by a lack of confidence in their ability to express themselves in writing.

—People who could perform important services in the organizations to which they belong fail to do so because they are afraid they would be unable to write minutes without spelling errors, or prepare clear reports to be read by their friends and associates.

—People who would otherwise engage in considerable correspondence are reluctant to do so; they realize that their errors in spelling will spoil the effect of whatever they want to write to others.

Spelling Self-Taught has been especially designed for these groups—for all who want to spell well.

The English language follows a large number of spelling rules. But, of course, *Spelling Self-Taught* does not include **all** of these rules. To do so would require a book several times the size of this one. *Spelling Self-Taught* recognizes some of the many exceptions to the rules it presents, but does not state all of the exceptions. It also contains many words in common use which cannot be learned by spelling rules.

But the road to correct spelling is a double one. First, you must learn the rules which will help you avoid most of the common spelling errors. Second, you must learn the special characteristics of those words which must be memorized. The rules included in this book are those which studies have shown to be most significant for the purposes of the average student or adult. The special words which have been selected because they have to be memorized are words whose correct spelling will mark you as someone who truly cares about what he writes.

The pages of this book contain the basic spelling vocabulary every person needs. The authors have distilled the learnings derived from their extensive experience in teaching children, adults and teachers. The result is a practical approach to the problem of avoiding common spelling errors.

How can you learn to spell? Correct spelling comes only with understanding and practice. You must learn rules; you must see correct spelling and recognize it; you must review what you have learned again and again. The group of review sections in *Spelling Self-Taught* is the key to teaching yourself how to spell well. There is a review at the end of each chapter. When you make errors in a review exercise, you should go back to the text and restudy the frames you have not yet mastered. In time, the reviews will become easier and easier. They provide the practice and personal testing you need to spell correctly.

Of course, the dictionary is the accepted authority for the correct spelling of any word. *Webster's New International Dictionary*, considered by many to be the most authoritative in the English language, has been selected as the basic authority for this book. *Webster's* often gives two or more spellings for a given word, with one of them indicated as preferable to the other. In *Spelling Self-Taught* secondary or "preferred" spellings are considered correct, even though the authors have not included them for study. When a spelling given in this book differs from one which you have previously learned, use the dictionary to check which is preferred.

How to Use This Book

You have probably already turned the pages of *Spelling Self-Taught*. It is different in appearance from any book you have ever read. Note that each page is divided into five sections. Each of these is called a "frame." Each frame is a short lesson or a short test. Each frame is a separate learning experience.

The method of presenting material in frames is called "programming." It is the method followed in many of the new teaching machines that are revolutionizing the entire field of education. The basic premise behind the program type of teaching is that you will learn quickly if each question you answer is followed at once by the correct answer. By giving you the right answer immediately, this book prevents your mind from fastening on an incorrect spelling. In short order you will find that all or most of your answers are correct. Programmed learning is highly efficient.

At What Speed Should You Work?

There are no time limits for the work in this book. If you work every day, you will progress rapidly. However, there are limits to the amount you can learn at a single sitting. You should try to work for half an hour or an hour at a time, not more often than once a day. Work at the speed that is most comfortable for you. You should be able to get through an entire chapter in one sitting. Then wait at least one day before you do any reviewing. Read through the questions and answers again before you do the chapter review.

Follow this system for each chapter. When you get to the middle of the book or beyond, you may find that you have forgotten some of the material covered in the earlier chapters. When that happens, go back to review that material before you go on with the book.

Before you begin, take the test on page 9, especially designed by the authors to help you measure your progress with *Spelling Self-Taught*. Take this test twice—once now and again after you have finished studying the book. Your improvement will be impressive—real proof of your hard work and of the efficiency of this specially designed teaching machine.

All you need for the test is a pen or pencil, a sheet of paper and the co-operation of a friend. Number from 1 to 25 on your paper. Then ask your friend to read each word aloud as well as the sentence which illustrates its use. Write each word. Of course, at the end of the test you will check your spellings against the correct ones.

If your score is 20 or more correct, then use this book as a general review of the spellings you should know. If it is between 15 and 19, you are only a fair speller. Use the book to learn or relearn the rules you do not know. But if your score is under 15, your spelling is poor. You should plan to spend several hours a week during the next few months working with this book.

SPELLING TEST

1. Plausible	His story was not very **plausible**.	Plausible
2. Secretary	Have you seen the new **secretary?**	Secretary
3. Dissatisfied	Why are you so **dissatisfied?**	Dissatisfied
4. Psychological	The book is a **psychological** study.	Psychological
5. Misspelled	The word has been **misspelled**.	Misspelled
6. Principle	Archimedes' **principle** should be mastered.	Principle
7. Succeed	You will **succeed** if you want to.	Succeed
8. Secede	The states wanted to **secede**.	Secede
9. Necessary	It is **necessary** to drive carefully.	Necessary
10. Principal	The **principal** figure is Holmes.	Principal
11. Stationery	This store sells candy and **stationery**.	Stationery
12. Manageable	The horse proved easily **manageable**.	Manageable
13. Occurrence	The fire was a tragic **occurrence**.	Occurrence
14. Stationary	My boss's desk is **stationary**.	Stationary
15. Receivable	The account is now **receivable**.	Receivable
16. Fluorescent	Most desk lamps are **fluorescent**.	Fluorescent
17. Exhilaration	I could not explain his **exhilaration**.	Exhilaration
18. Independent	At last he has become **indcpendent**.	Independent
19. Superintendent	Is your **superintendent** efficient?	Superintendent
20. Miscellaneous	He sells **miscellaneous** items at home.	Miscellaneous
21. Contemptible	It was a **contemptible** action.	Contemptible
22. Temperament	Many singers are fiery by **temperament**.	Temperament
23. Accommodate	How many people will the car **accommodate?**	Accommodate
24. Eighth	Is he **eighth** or ninth in line?	Eighth
25. Ecstasy	Her happiness was close to **ecstasy**.	Ecstasy

Do not try to rush through *Spelling Self-Taught*. You have to correct the bad habits of a lifetime. Expect to spend at least a few months to become a more competent speller. Remember that the correction of error is your goal, and that repetition and review are necessary to achieve that goal.

And now you are ready to begin *Spelling Self-Taught!*

HOW TO USE "SPELLING SELF-TAUGHT"

Look at the page of frames to your right. Note that the top frame, which is blue, has the number 1 in its lower right-hand corner. The frame ends with a question. Write the answer to this question on a sheet of paper.

Now, turn the page. For the time being, pay no attention to page 12. You will work first through the odd-numbered pages and later through the even-numbered left-hand pages. At the top of page 13 you will see Frame 2, and on its left the answer to Frame 1. If you answered Frame 1 correctly, go on and write down your answers to the questions in Frame 2.

This is the way you will work through the book. Of course, when you make a mistake, you should restudy the frame involved. Stop whenever you miss a question. Go back to the previous frame or group of frames to see why you are incorrect. Never go ahead unless you are certain you understand everything that has gone before!

When you reach the last page in the book, the top right-hand frame will be 59. To find Frame 60, turn back to page 11. Frame 60 is the second one from the top of page 11. Proceed in this way until you have finished all the right-hand pages in the book. Of course, the answers to whatever frame you are working on, will always be on the left of the next frame in order. As soon as you have finished all the right-hand pages (or Frame 295), you are ready to begin working on the left-hand pages. Turn back to page 12, and you will see Frame 296 at the top.

Remember! Work at a leisurely pace, and do not take on new material until you have mastered the old!

I. THE APPROACH TO SPELLING

To spell a word correctly, you must:
Listen to the word, **look** at the word, and **say** the word.
Say these words and **listen** to the sounds:

      retract   **popular**   **president**

Will you spell every sound you **say** in these words? **1**

---

tolerance

Suffixes

Select the correct form.
a) A person who toler**ates** something is said to be **(tolerent . . . tolerant).**
b) If you domin**ate,** you are said to be a **(dominant . . . dominent)** person.
c) Do not hesit**ate** means to show no **(hesitance . . . hesitence).** **60**

---

a) forcing

b) shining

Before a Suffix Starting with a Vowel

Find the five **incorrectly** spelled words in dark type, and write them correctly.
I am **encloseing** the **useable clothing** you requested. John is not as careless as he used to be, and isn't **loseing** buttons as he once did. However, his **insistence** on **chaseing** rabbits is **causeing** me great worry, for he is often **teased** about it. **119**

---

a) copying

b) copies

c) trying

d) families

Final Y Following a Consonant

Select and correct the three designated words that arc incorrectly spelled.
I was certain that I could do the job **easly.** I **applied** the paint, but tipped the container while **appliing** it. My **beautiful** plan was spoiled, and I was soon **busyly** cleaning up the mess I had made. **178**

---

a) shipped

b) rubbing

c) happily

    dragged

d) robbed

Doubling the Final Consonant

Select the correct word:
a) This is the **(hottest, hotest)** day I have ever known.
b) When are the soldiers **(comming, coming),** sir?
c) Aladdin did not realize what would happen when he **(rubed, rubbed)** the magic lamp. **237**

Nouns Ending in F or FE

Select the correct word:
a) It was the best year of their (lifes, lives).
b) The sailors thronged the (wharves, wharfs).
c) They kept it all for (themselfs, themselves).
d) The cakes were cut into (halves, halfs).
e) Where is the school for (chefs, cheves)?

296

a) niece

b) brief

c) interview

d) Hygiene

e) overweight

What Have You Learned?

a) Is your home a **residence** or a **residance**?
b) Is the woman next door a **nieghbor** or a **neighbor**?
c) With the extra room, our crowded condition was very much **(releived, relieved)**.
d) At last we can entertain our **(freinds, friends)**.

354

The Sounds of GH

Can you hear the **gh** in **higher?**
Rule: The **gh** is silent when it follows the letter **i** in the same syllable.
In the words **high** and **higher**, the gh follows an **i**, the letters h-i-g-h form a single syllable. The sound of **gh** in **high** and **higher** is therefore **(silent, heard)**.

412

a) their

b) there

c) they're

two, to, and too

Two is the number. **To** is a preposition used to show a direction or connection. **Too** means "in addition to," or "also."
a) I want **(two, to, too)** join the **(two, to, too)** men in the office.
b) You **(two, to, too)** boys have to go to sleep **(two, to, too)**.

470

a) mail

b) males

mail

minor and miner

A **minor** is one under legal age; a **miner** is one who works in a mine. **Minor** also refers to something relatively insignificant.
a) Divide your conclusions into major and **(miner, minor)** groups.
b) **(Minors, Miners)** cannot be employed as **(minors, miners)**.

528

12

SPELLING BY SOUND

Look at these words carefully. Do you see something special about each of them?

yes

Manhattan   **psychology**

a) Which word can be divided into three small words?

b) Which word has two silent letters?

2

Suffixes

a) tolerant

b) dominant

c) hesitance

Select the correct form.

a) Anything which exists is said to be exist**ent**. You cannot therefore deny its **(existence, existance)**.

b) A prud**ent** person is one who is very careful in all things, thereby proving his **(prudance, prudence)**.

c) A pati**ent** man has great **(patience, patiance)**.

61

Before a Suffix Starting with a Vowel

enclosing

usable

losing

chasing

causing

Add the suffix **-er** to each of the words below:

a) **Pale** plus -**er** becomes ....

b) **Rude** plus -**er** becomes ....

c) **Choke** plus -**er** becomes ....

d) **Love** plus -**er** becomes ....

e) **Divide** plus -**er** becomes ....

120

Review

easily

applying

busily

Find and correct the six incorrect spellings in the list of words below:

fryed	impatiance	rosyest	lazyer
applying	happily	prying	insistence
admirible	flying	carryed	baking

179

Doubling the Final Consonant

a) hottest

b) coming

c) rubbed

Select the correct word:

a) The sudden smoke **(blured, blurred)** his vision.

b) She **(stared, starred)** as the heroine of the film.

c) This low-calorie diet should make you **(slimer, slimmer)**.

d) The **(robber, rober)** made away with the crown jewels.

238

13

a) lives

b) wharves

c) themselves

d) halves

e) chefs

Nouns Ending in F or FE

Did you note that the correct answer was **chefs**, not **cheves**? There are many words which end in -f or -fe which do not change the **f** to a **v**. You must remember that the "rule" we are studying is a **sometimes** rule. The next few frames will give you some practice with it.

Which is correct, **loafs** or **loaves**?

297

---

a) residence

b) neighbor

c) relieved

d) friends

What Have You Learned?

a) The Smiths live in an **(efficeincy, efficiency)** apartment down the street.

b) The magician was gifted with an **(incredable, incredible)** talent for **(slieght-of-hand, sleight-of-hand)** tricks.

c) His past record is not **(relevent, relevant)**.

355

---

silent

The Sounds of GH

Practice with the **igh** combination:

a) Is the **gh** silent or sounded in the word **light**?

b) Can you hear the **gh** in the word **frighten**?

c) Is the **gh** silent in the word **pigheaded**?

d) In the word **sight** the gh is **(silent, sounded)**.

e) In the word **bighearted**, the gh is **(silent, sounded)**.

413

---

a) to

two

b) two

too

week and weak

Week refers to the unit of time equal to seven days.

Weak refers to a lack of strength or ability.

a) The wrestler displayed unexpected **(weekness, weakness)**.

b) The mail is delivered **(weakly, weekly)**.

c) After seven days, the horse had **(weekened, weakened)**.

471

---

a) minor

b) Minors

miners

Select the correct word:

a) I need a strong **(male, mail)** to post this heavy **(mail, male)**.

b) I am convinced this liquid is **(lie, lye)**.

c) He was happy when the speaker **(sighted, cited)** his work.

d) The explorers agreed that the **(assent, ascent)** was possible.

529

Spelling by Sound

Now LOOK at these words and say them aloud:

facetiously   rarefy

a) Which word has all the six vowels the way you learned to say them in alphabetical order— **a, e, i, o, u, y**?

b) Does the second word have two or three syllables?

3

---

innocent or **innocant?**
significant or **significent?**
innocence or **innocance?**

When should the suffix begin with **a** and when should it begin with **e**? The answer depends upon the root form of the word. In general, the kind of sound in the root word will tell you the kind of suffix that goes with it.

62

Before a Suffix Starting with a Vowel

Add the suffix **-ed** to each of the words below:
a) **Fine** plus -ed becomes ....
b) **Praise** plus -ed becomes ....
c) **Refuse** plus -ed becomes ....
d) **Hate** plus -ed becomes ....
e) **Promise** plus -ed becomes ....

121

Final Y Following a Consonant

Remember the rule: Final **y** becomes **i.**
a) The princess and the commoner were soon **(marryed, married).**
b) The happy father rushed off to purchase a baby **(carryage, carriage).**

180

Doubling the Final Consonant

Select the correct word:
a) Which of the following does not come from **bet: betting, beter?** Correct the misspelled word.
b) The past form of **grip** is **(griped, gripped).**
c) The past form of **gripe** is **(griped, gripped).**

239

Nouns Ending in F or FE

Select the correct word:

loaves

a) She admired the color of the autumn **(leafs, leaves)**.

b) It was a fairy tale about three happy **(elfs, elves)**.

c) The cows milled about seeking their **(calfs, calves)**.

d) The ships foundered on the **(reefs, reeves)**. **298**

---

a) efficiency

b) incredible

    sleight-of-hand

c) relevant

REVIEW (IX)

a) The ground was covered by **(leafs, leaves)**.

b) The threat of checkmate forced the chess master to **(yeild, yield)**.

c) Do not deliver the goods unless you receive a properly signed **(receipt, reciept)**.

356

---

a) silent

b) no

c) no

d) silent

e) sounded

The Sounds of GH

Can you hear the **gh** in **ghost**?

Rule: The **gh** combination at the beginning of most words has the sound of **g** in **gun**. The addition of a one-letter prefix such as **a-** does not change the hard **g** sound of an initial **gh**.

What is the sound of the **gh** in **ghost**?

414

Homonyms

weather and whether

a) weakness

b) weekly

c) weakened

Weather refers to the condition of the atmosphere.

Whether is used to indicate a choice between alternatives when a state of doubt or uncertainty exists.

a) The rocket was sent aloft to help determine the future pattern of the **(whether, weather)**.

b) I will go **(whether, weather)** or not it rains. **472**

Homonyms

a) male

    mail

b) lye

c) cited

d) ascent

pain and pane

Pain is physical discomfort or distress; **pane** refers to a sheet of glass, like that in a window.

a) It **(pained, paned)** me to see him break the valuable sheet of glass.

b) Now I know how to install a new **(pain, pane)**. **530**

16

a) facetiously

b) 3
rar-e-fy

It's important in spelling to remember that the vowels are **a, e, i, o** and **u**. When **y** takes the place of i, as in **typical** or **analysis**, it is considered a vowel, too. You will also see later how helpful it is to be able to break a word into syllables. In spelling, you will often find silent letters. But much of the time, you will be able to spell a word correctly if you pronounce it correctly.

4

Suffixes

Does the suffix begin with **a** or **e**?
Rule 1: If the root ends with a soft **c** or a soft **g**, the suffix will probably begin with an **e**. In the word **innocent,** the **c** is soft. (A hard **c** would have the sound of **k** as in cat.)
Which is correct, **innocence** or **innocance?**

63

a) fined

b) praised

c) refused

d) hated

e) promised

BEFORE A SUFFIX STARTING WITH A CONSONANT

Rule: Keep the final **e** when you add a suffix beginning with a consonant.
a) Adding **-less** to the word **care** makes the word
....
b) Adding **-ly** to the word **complete** makes............
c) The combination of **replace** and **-ment** is
....

122

Final Y Following a Consonant

What happens to the final **y**?

a) married

b) carriage

a) Come, oh come, and see the **(mysteryous, mysterious)** land of Oz!
b) The **(studious, studyous)** pupil was diligent, and his **(diligence, diligance)** was rewarded.
c) How **(busyly, busily)** the busy bees go about their **(busyness, business)!**

181

Doubling the Final Consonant

a) better

b) gripped

c) griped

Select the correct word:
a) If you are doing some carpentry, you are **(planing, planning).**
b) One who commits a **sin** is a **(siner, sinner).**
c) The horse would not run fast unless he were severely **(whiped, whipped).**
d) Is a person who **dines** a **(diner** or a **dinner)?**

240

17

Nouns Ending in F or FE

a) leaves

b) elves

c) calves

d) reefs

Correct the misspelled word in each group.
a) elves   selves   chievcs   loaves
b) chefs   serfs   wolfs   cuffs
c) handkerchiefs   gulfs   wharfs   sheriffs
d) muffs   proofs   wives   rooves
e) gulves   reefs   fifes   waifs

299

Review (IX)

a) leaves

b) yield

c) receipt

a) I cannot understand why you are so surly and (arguementative, argumentative).
b) Do not be so (persistant, persistent).
c) I abhor the hateful scenes which my upbringing has taught me to consider (abhorent, abhorrent).

357

The Sounds of GH

hard g

a) Which word in this group contains a silent gh?
  ghastly   aghast   right   ghostly
b) Which word in this group has the hard g sound?
  frightened   mighty   ghetto   tightened
c) In ghoul, a folklore creature believed to rob graves, the gh is (silent, heard)?

415

which and witch

a) weather

b) whether

Which is used to indicate one or more of a number of things or persons. Witch refers to a woman believed to possess special powers through a compact with evil forces.
a) (Which, Witch) of these women is the (which, witch)?
b) The dog ran as if (bewhiched, bewitched).

473

so, sew and sow

a) pained

b) pane

So indicates an extreme of some sort, as "so many," or "so few." It is also used as a connective. "To sew" is to use needle and thread. To sow is to plant.
a) Why are (so, sew, sow) many people here today?
b) Who (sewed, sowed) the seeds of discontent among the (sowing, sewing) girls at the factory?

531

18

Spelling by Sound

A vowel is called **silent** when you do not hear it in pronouncing the word. For example, the letter **e** is silent in:

    pine   **fire**   **bite**   **rate**   **fare**   **pane**

If you left off the **e** in these words, would you pronounce the words the same?

5

---

innocence

Suffixes

Rule 1: Use the suffix beginning with **e** after a soft **c** or **g.**

a) Which is correct, **intelligence** or **intelligance?**
b) Which is correct, **magnificant** or **magnificent?**
c) Is a careless person **negligant** or **negligent?**

64

---

a) careless

b) completely

c) replacement

Before a Suffix Starting with a Consonant

Correct the misspelled word in each group of words:

a) **nicely closeness casement latly**
b) **sincerely lonely rarly actively**
c) **firelike fineness gratful definitely**
d) **ninty definiteness finitely requirements**

123

---

a) mysterious

b) studious

    diligence

c) busily

    business

Final Y Following a Consonant

What happens to the final **y?**

a) I cannot understand why you are **(worriing, worrying).**
b) He is a notorious criminal who was not to be trusted, even while **(testifying, testifiing).**
c) The ghostly figure **(ferried, ferryed)** them home.

182

---

a) planing

b) sinner

c) whipped

d) diner

Doubling the Final Consonant

Select the correct word:

a) And does he dine in a **dinning** room or a **dining** room?
b) The meal he eats is, of course, his **(diner, dinner).**
c) Hot? Why, it has never been **(hotter, hoter)!**
d) Are you really **(succeedding, succeeding)?**

241

19

Nouns Ending in F or FE
Does **cliff** become **clives?**

a) chiefs

b) wolves

c) wharves

d) roofs

e) gulfs

The ending **ff** usually means that the plural is formed by adding an **s**. There is usually no change of **f** to **v**.

a) The plural of **bluff** would thus be (**bluffs, bluves**).

b) A tariff law deals with (**tarives, tariffs**).

c) Some court officials are called (**bailiffs, bailives**).

300

Review (IX)

a) argumentative

b) persistent

c) abhorrent

Reminder: The answer in Frame 357 was **abhorrent** for two reasons:

a) The final **r** was doubled before the addition of a suffix beginning with a vowel.

b) Since the accent is on the last syllable of **abhor**, it takes the ending **-ent**.

358

Some silent **gh** combinations:

a) right

b) ghetto

c) heard as a hard **g**

The **gh** is silent in these words and in those made from them:

though	bough	dough	taught	daughter
thought	bought	aught	caught	slaughter
sought	brought	nought	fraught	wrought

These are the most common silent **gh** words in which the **gh** follows the combination **au** or **ou**.

416

---

whole and **hole**

a) Which

witch

b) bewitched

Whole indicates all of something, its entirety. A **hole** is a place that has been rounded or hollowed out.

a) The (**hole-wheat, whole-wheat**) bread is baked here.

b) Swiss cheese is characterized by its (**wholes, holes**).

474

---

vein, vain and **vane**

a) so

b) sowed

sewing

A **vein** is a blood vessel, or a layer or trace of an ore. The word **vain**, used in the form **in vain**, functions as an adverb and means useless. But usually **vain** means conceited or self-centered. A **vane** is found on a windmill or propeller. The word **vein** is also used to describe the general tone of something: for example, "in a satiric vein."

532

Spelling by Sound

no

Of course, you would not. Compare:
   pin and **pine**   **bit** and **bite**   **rat** and **rate**
What does the **e** do? It affects the sound of the preceding vowel, and changes it from short to long.

6

---

a) intelligence

b) magnificent

c) negligent

Suffixes

a) Are two things close together **adjacant** or **adjacent?**

b) Is a teen-ager an **adolescent** or an **adolescant?**

65

---

a) lately

b) rarely

c) grateful

d) ninety

Final Silent E Before a Suffix

Find and correct the four misspelled words.
It was a wonderful day! The **lateness** of the hour **scarcly** mattered, for the **shineing** sun still cast its **forcful** light upon us. We were **absolutely** overjoyed by the sight of a **lovly** group of gulls flying nearby.

124

---

a) worrying

b) testifying

c) ferried

EXCEPTIONS TO THE RULE: TO BE MEMORIZED

   day—daily say—said slay—slain
   pay—paid lay—laid

These five pairs of words do not follow the rule we have been studying. You must memorize them.

183

---

a) dining

b) dinner

c) hotter

d) succeeding

Doubling the Final Consonant

Select the correct word:
a) Why is your dog **(barkking, barking)**?
b) Is it because you haven't **(pated, patted)** him?
c) No, it is his fear of the **(firing, firring)** guns.
d) Enough of your **(puning, punning),** my funny
    friend!

242

Nouns Ending in F or FE

a) bluffs

b) tariffs

c) bailiffs

Select the correct word:
a) She selected two lovely (**scarfs, scarves**).
b) Be careful of the horse's (**hoofs, hooves**).
c) How many (**sheafs, sheaves**) of wheat are there?
d) The artist viewed the city from its (**rooves, roofs**).
e) Place the books on the proper (**shelfs, shelves**).

301

Review (IX)

a) When you permit an accident to occur, you are guilty of contributory (**negligance, negligence**).
b) Is a man who is demoted **superceded** or **superseded**?
c) One character in the film had three (**fezes, fezzes**).

359

The Sounds of GH

a) Which of these words has a silent **gh**?
    aghast   **ghostly**   **thought**   **gherkin**
b) Which of these words has a sounded **gh**?
    slaughter   **dough**   **wrought**   **ghoulish**
c) Which word contains the greatest number of silent letters?
    slaughter   **wrought**   **thoughtful**   **untaught**

417

Homonyms

a) whole-wheat

b) holes

Correct the five **misspelled** words in this paragraph. He had spent his hole life in this cottage near the Straights of Gibraltar. It was a pieceful existence with the quiet sheep grazing their on the hill. In the end, weekened by a sudden attack of the plague, he died.

475

Homonyms

Select the correct word:
a) The (**minor, miner**) was elated when he found a rich (**vein, vane, vain**) of ore.
b) He had searched for it for years in (**vein, vain**).
c) The (**veins, vanes**) of the propeller moved slowly.

533

22

Spelling by Sound

When you say the vowels exactly as you say **a, e, i, o, u** and sometimes **y**, you are pronouncing **long vowels**. Otherwise, they are usually short. Select the words below with long vowels:

     grape   **fine**   **pin**   **hurt**

7

Suffixes

a) adjacent

b) adolescent

Does the suffix begin with **e** or **a**?
Rule 2: If the root ends in **-sist** or **-xist**, the ending or suffix will probably be **-ence** or **-ent**.
Existence or **existance**? **Existence** is correct because the root is **exist**, ending in **-xist**.
Consistant or **consistent**? **Consistent** is correct because the root is **consist**, ending in **-sist**.

66

Final Silent E Before a Suffix

scarcely

shining

forceful

lovely

Find and correct the four misspelled words.
The space ship was launched at **precisly** the agreed hour, and **dissappeared** from sight in less than a minute. Were we to be **disappointed** at the failure of this **incredable** flight, or would its return bring **definitly** greater joy than we had believed **imaginable**?

125

Exceptions

Select the correct word:
a) What are you (**saying, saiing**)?
b) You heard what I (**sayed, said**).
c) The bills are now (**paiable, payable**).
d) She will be so happy when those bills are (**payed, paid**).
e) His (**dayly, daily**) newspaper arrived late.

184

WORDS OF MORE THAN ONE SYLLABLE ENDING IN A SINGLE CONSONANT PRECEDED BY A SINGLE VOWEL

a) barking

b) patted

c) firing

d) punning

Rule: If a word ending in a vowel followed by a consonant has more than one syllable, and it is accented on its last syllable, **double the final consonant** before adding an ending that begins with a vowel.

243

Nouns Ending in F or FE

a) scarves
b) hoofs
c) sheaves
d) roofs
e) shelves

Correct the four misspelled words:
It was a time for action, and the **serfs** were not long in blowing their **fives** and sounding their horns. The **lifes** of those men who acted like **wolfs** would not be spared. Even the little **waifs** joined the screaming mob that moved upon the **chieves** of the hated prison.

302

Review (IX)

a) negligence
b) superseded
c) fezzes

a) The horse approached (**shily, shyly**).
b) **Heavy** combined with **-ness** makes ....
c) Is it **fanciest** or **fancyest**?
d) Is it **copyer** or **copier**?

360

The Sounds of GH

a) thought
b) ghoulish
c) wrought

When **gh** equals **f**.
The sound of **gh** is the sound of **f** (as in **cuff**) in these words and those made from them.
    laugh cough tough rough enough trough

418

Homonyms

whole
Straits
peaceful
there
weakened

Select the correct word:
a) The parson was (**holy, wholly**) correct.
b) The words reminded them of some strange (**whichery, witchery**).
c) The navigator did not know (**weather, whether**) to sail on or turn around.

476

Homonyms

a) miner
   vein
b) vain
c) vanes

February or **Febuary**? **Library** or **libary**?
These words are not homonyms, for one of each pair is a mispronunciation. If you remember to pronounce the first **r** in each word, then you will know that the correct spellings are **February** and **Library**.

534

Spelling by Sound

grape

fine

If you heard these sounds, how would you spell the words they form?

a) c—long o—n .... **con** or **cone?**
b) p—long u—r .... **purr** or **pure?**
c) f—short a—t .... **fat** or **fate?**

8

Suffixes

Does the suffix begin with **e** or **a?**

a) Is a person who insists **insistant** or **insistent?**
b) If you persist in something, are you **persistent** or **persistant?**
c) If your salary is just enough to subsist on, is it a **subsistance** wage or a **subsistence** wage?

67

Before a Suffix Starting with a Consonant

precisely

disappeared

incredible

definitely

Add the suffix to each of the words below:

a) **sure** plus **-ly** becomes ....
b) **rare** plus **-ly** becomes ....
c) **fine** plus **-ness** becomes ....
d) **late** plus **-ness** becomes ....
e) **close** plus **-ness** becomes ....

126

Review, the Final Y

a) saying

b) said

c) payable

d) paid

e) daily

Select the correct word:

a) How wonderful! The chicken **(laid, layed)** an egg.
b) John and Mary **(played, plaid)** with the children.
c) The people were sad when their leader was **(slayn, slain)**.
d) It is a debt which will never be **(payed, paid)**.

185

beginer or beginner?   refered or referred?

a) The word **begin** has two syllables (be-gin). The accented syllable is the last one, **-gin**. You therefore double the final consonant before adding **-er**.
The correct form is **(beginer, beginner)**.
b) **Refer** has its accent on its last syllable, and becomes **(refered, referred)**.

244

25

	Nouns Ending in F or FE
fifes	Which two sentences contain errors? What errors?
lives	*a*) The wives, with scarves flying, crowded the wharves.
wolves	*b*) The chiefs burned the leafs near the reefs.
	c) The elves built the shelves for themselves.
chiefs	*d*) The prints of the hoofs were on the roofs.
	e) The chefs baked the loafs for the serfs. **303**

X. DON'T LET THE SOUND CONFUSE YOU

a) shyly

b) heaviness

c) fanciest

d) copier

This chapter deals with some of the sounds you hear and do not hear in the English language. Practice is essential, for much of what follows will have to be memorized. Work slowly. Stop frequently and go back to the first frames of this chapter—when you have missed a question.   **361**

The Sounds of GH

a) What is the sound of the **gh** in **laughter?**
b) What is the sound of the **gh** in **coughing?**
c) Can you hear the **gh** in **caught?**
d) In the word **roughness,** the **gh** has the sound of....

419

Homonyms

a) wholly

b) witchery

c) whether

wrote and **rote**

Wrote is the past form of the verb **write. Rote** refers to a fixed way of doing something, often to memorizing.

a) Who **(rote, wrote)** this set of rules?
b) The children learned their multiplication tables by **(wrote, rote).**   **477**

XII. COMMONLY MISSPELLED WORDS

This final chapter contains practice in spelling special words which are found among those most commonly misspelled. These words have special features of difficulty.

First, do the questions in each frame before learning the listed words. Check your answers against the correct spellings. Try the questions again.   **535**

Spelling by Sound

a) cone

b) pure

c) fat

The letters which are not vowels are called **consonants**. Usually, each consonant represents one sound, but sometimes two consonants combined make only one sound. Less often, one consonant stands for two sounds. It's easy to find the consonants in each of these words:

strict   **problems**   **example**   **9**

Suffixes

a) insistent

b) persistent

c) subsistence

Does the suffix begin with **e** or **a**?

a) If you refuse to give up in your efforts to solve a problem, are you showing **persistence** or **persistance**?

b) The act of insisting is called **(insistance, insistence)**.

c) Something which is **(subsistent, subsistant)** is real. **68**

Before a Suffix Starting with a Consonant

a) surely

b) rarely

c) fineness

d) lateness

e) closeness

Add the suffix **-ment** to each of the words below:

a) **induce** combined with **-ment** gives...................

b) **place** combined with **-ment** gives ....

c) **manage** combined with **-ment** gives.................

d) **base** combined with **-ment** gives..................

e) **amuse** combined with **-ment** gives **127**

a) laid

b) played

c) slain

d) paid

Select the correct word:

a) Those words had better remain **(unsayed, unsaid)**.

b) The city of Syracuse was heavily **(fortifyed, fortified)**.

c) At long last, my enemy has been **(repayed, repaid)**.

d) I remember when Italy was an **(occupied, occupyed)** country. **186**

a) beginner

b) referred

a) The word **depart** has two syllables (de-part). The accent is on the **last** syllable. However, it does **not** end with one vowel followed by one consonant. The rule does not apply, and the correct form is **(departted, departed)**.

b) The rule does apply when **forgot** becomes **(forgoten, forgotten)**. **245**

27

b) and *e*

leaves

loaves

Nouns Ending in F or FE
Which of these sentences is correct?
a) The wolves tore the loaves into halfs.
b) The leaves fell upon the bluffs and cliffs.
c) He learned his proofs with diligence.
d) The gulfs were fed by navigible rivers.

304

WHEN CH SOUNDS LIKE K
chemistry or kemistry?
Certain consonant sounds are represented by other letters. The word **chemistry** has the initial **k** sound. All other words with the **ch** root from the Greek are also spelled with the **ch** for the **k** sound. Is it **character** or **karacter?**

362

a) **f**

b) **f**

c) no

d) **f**

The Sounds of GH
Which word in each group has a **gh** sound different from that of the other words?
a) **laugh   laughing   laughed   daughter**
b) **bright   delight   ghost   slightly**
c) **through   bough   rough   dough**
d) **taught   brought   slaughter   enough**

420

Homonyms
all together and altogether
a) wrote

b) rote
Use **all together** when you refer to many things or people in the same place. Use **altogether** when you mean **completely** or **entirely**.
a) The diagnosis was **(all together, altogether)** faulty.
b) The prisoners were **(all together, altogether).**   478

Test yourself by trying the questions **before** you look at the correctly spelled words. Cover them. Select the correct spellings:
    across   amateur   apparent   appreciate
a) Please walk **(accros, across)** the room.
b) The solution is quite **(aparant, aparent, apparent).**
c) I **(apreshiate, appreshiate, appreciate)** your interest.   536

28

Spelling by Sound

a) s, t, r, c, t

b) p, r, b, l, m, s

c) x, m, p, l

Sometimes a consonant represents **two** sounds. Look at these three words:

    tax   excuse   oxen

a) What consonant in each word represents two sounds?

b) Which sounds does it represent?

10

An exception to Rule 2: resist.

a) persistence

b) insistence

c) subsistent

English spelling follows certain rules, but it also contains many exceptions to these rules. The exceptions must be memorized. **Resist** is an exception to Rule 2, Frame 66. It ends in **-sist,** but uses suffixes beginning with **a.**

Which are correct: **(resistent, resistant); (resistance, resistence)?**

69

---

a) inducement

b) placement

c) management

d) basement

e) amusement

The designated words are root words, to which you are to add **-ly, -ness,** or **-ment,** selecting the ending which makes the most sense.

I **bare**......... managed to reach the **base**......... when the storm struck. I had **sure**......... been lucky, for the **close**......... of my escape was indicated by the **definite**............ crashing timbers on the floor above.

128

Review, the Final Y

a) unsaid

b) fortified

c) repaid

d) occupied

Select the correct word:

a) How have you **(justified, justifyed)** your actions?

b) From what **(countrys, countries)** did they come?

c) You must admit that he **(trys, tries)** to do well.

d) Beware! There is danger that you will be **(slayn, slain).**

187

Doubling the Final Consonant

a) departed

b) forgotten

Select the correct word:

a) The event **(occured, occurred)** long ago.

b) It was a curious **(occurrence, occurence).**

c) How completely is your auto **(equiped, equipped)?**

d) The government of the dictatorship **(controled, controlled)** every aspect of production.

246

Review

Correct the errors in these sentences. One sentence is correct as it is.

a) Attempt no resistence to the sheriffs!

b) The thieves superseded the host's authority.

c) The sultan's wives masked themselves with scarfs.

305

character

When CH Sounds Like K

More words in which **ch** sounds like **k**.
Select the correct word:

a) Play the first of these **(chords, kords)**.

b) He is a professor of **(biokemistry, biochemistry)**.

c) Now for the **(kemical, chemical)** reaction!

d) The animal was a **(kameleon, chameleon)**.

363

a) daughter

b) ghost

c) rough

d) enough

THE SILENT D

Rule: The letter **d** when followed by the **j** sound is silent. The **dg** or **dj** combination has the sound of **j**.

a) The sound of the consonants in **edge** is **(dj, j)**.

b) The **d** in **adjust** is **(silent, sounded)**.

421

Homonyms

a) altogether

b) all together

clothes and **close**

Clothes refers to the garments you wear. **Close,** on the other hand, is a verb meaning "to shut."
My **(close, clothes)** are made of fine fabrics.

479

Select the correct spellings.

appetite   athletics   banana   beneficial

a) across

b) apparent

c) appreciate

a) He has a healthy **(apetight, appetite, apetite)**.

b) He earned fame for his skill in **(athletics, atheletics)**.

c) This ice cream dish is called a **(benana, banana)** split.

d) I trust the sunshine will be **(beneficial, benificial)**.

537

a) x

b) ks

Spelling by Sound

Often two consonants together equal only one sound. Look at these two words:

cough　　　**indebted**

a) In each word what consonants represent only one sound?

b) Which sounds are represented in each case?

11

VERB SUFFIXES

Reminder: What is a verb?

resistant

resistance

A verb is a word which expresses an action or a state of being. Many words are formed from roots which are verbs. Can you recognize the verb which is the root of each of the following words?

jumper　　**refusal**　　**improvement**　　**denial**

70

barely

basement

surely

closeness

definitely

FINAL SILENT E AFTER SOFT C OR G

arrangeable or **arrangable**; **serviceable** or **servicable**

Rule: When a word ends in a soft **c** or a soft **g** (as in **range**), followed by a silent **e**, **keep** the final **e** when adding a suffix beginning with **a** or **o**.

129

Review, the Final Y

a) justified

b) countries

c) tries

d) slain

Select the correct word:

a) The thief was captured while (**buriing, burying**) his loot.

b) If you are lonely, remember that (**lonelyness, loneliness**) will end when you join our group.

c) She says her prayers (**dayly, daily**).

188

a) occurred

b) occurrence

c) equipped

d) controlled

Select the correct word:

a) I could not understand why he (**prefered, preferred**) onion soup until he (**explained, explainned**).

b) The water is still (**boilling, boiling**).

c) The radio operator was proud of his new (**transmiter, transmitter**), and showed it to the visiting sailors.

247

SOME IRREGULAR PLURALS

a) resistance

c) scarves

There are some words which follow no rules at all in the formation of their plurals. Some of the more common ones are:

**child—children   man—men   foot-feet   ox-oxen
mouse—mice louse—lice tooth—teeth goose—geese**

306

When CH Sounds Like K

a) chords

b) biochemistry

c) chemical

d) chameleon

Another group of words in which **ch** sounds like **k.**

technical	**saccharine**
psychology	**choral**
pachyderm	**Christian**
chlorine	**chronology**

In most other words containing the **ch,** the sound is **ch** as in **child,** or **sh** as in **Charlotte.**   **364**

The Silent D

a) j

b) silent

Practice with **dg** and **dj.**
a) In which of these words is the sound of **dg** a **j**?
   Edgar   ledger   head-guard   sledge
b) The sound of **dj** in adjourn is **(silent, dj, j).**
c) What is the silent letter in each of these words?
   badger   hedges   adjusted   judging   422

Homonyms   course and coarse

clothes

A **course** is both a path of action and a unit of study. It is also a verb which means "to move quickly." When used in the expression **of course,** it means "as expected." The word **coarse** means rough or crude.
a) Of **(coarse, course)** I passed the **(coarse, course).**
b) The sergeant has a very **(coarse, course)** manner.

480

---

a) appetite

b) athletics

c) banana

d) beneficial

Select the correct spellings.
   association   bargain   biscuit   cafeteria
a) I had lunch at the **(cafateria, cafeteria, cafeterier).**
b) Please pass the **(biskits, biscuts, biscuits).**
c) Will you join our **(asociation, association, assosiation)?**
d) I think this dress is a **(bargin, bargian, bargain).**

538

a) gh

　bt

b) f

　t

Spelling by Sound

Here are some other words which show how two consonants combine to make only one sound.

telephone　　telegraph　　physics

a) What sound is represented by two letters in each word?

b) What are the letters which represent this sound? **12**

---

jump

refuse

improve

deny

Verb Suffixes

-ence and -ent: confer becomes conference.
Rule 3: If the original form of the word is a verb, and the final syllable of this verb is accented, **and** the verb ends with a vowel followed by an **r**, then the suffix will be **-ence** or **-ent**.

71

Final Silent E after Soft C or G

arrangeable or arrangable?

The word **arrange** ends in a soft **g** followed by a silent **e**. The suffix **-able** begins with an **a**. The correct spelling is therefore ....

130

---

a) burying

b) loneliness

c) daily

ONE-SYLLABLE ADJECTIVES ENDING IN Y

sly+ly=slyly　　dry+ly=dryly

Rule: For an adjective of one syllable, ending in a consonant followed by a **y**, keep the **y** before you add **-ly** to make an adverb, or **-ness** to make a noun from the adjective.

189

---

a) preferred

　explained

b) boiling

c) transmitter

Did you make a mistake with the word **explained** in Frame 247? At first glance, it would seem to be a word that follows the rule about doubling final consonants. When you look at **explain** again, you see that it ends with **two** vowels followed by a consonant. In such cases, you do not double the final consonant.

248

Irregular Plurals

Select the correct word:
a) The mother obviously loved her **(childs, children)**.
b) He had cut himself on both **(foots, feet)**.
c) There in the sky was a flock of **(geese, gooses)**.
d) The wagon was pulled by a team of **(oxes, oxen)**.
e) The dog was infested with **(louses, lice)**.

307

When CH Sounds Like K

Which word in each group has the sound **k** in it?
a) **hatchet   charming   chorus   chum**
b) **enchant   chromatic   itching   choose**
c) **characteristic   chill   champion   churl**
d) **chocolate   chopping   chosen   cholesterol**

365

a) ledger	**THE SILENT T**
	Can you hear the **t** in **listen?** in **start?**
sledge	*a*) The **t** in the word **listen** is part of an **st** combination in the middle of a word. It is therefore **(silent, sounded)**.
b) j	
c) d	*b*) The **t**'s in the word **start** are near the beginning and at the end of the word. They are therefore **(silent, sounded)**. 423

Homonyms

it's and **its**

a) course

course

b) coarse

It's is a contraction which means **"it is."** Its is the possessive form of the pronoun **it** and means "belonging to it."
a) **(It's Its)** tail began wagging when the little dog saw **(it's its)** master.
b) **(It's Its)** a fine day for hiking!

481

a) cafeteria

b) biscuits

c) association

d) bargain

Cover the correct spellings before doing the questions.
Select the correct spellings.
bookkeeper   calendar   campaign
a) The nomination was followed by the **(campaign, campane)**.
b) Susan is working as a **(bookeeper, bookkeeper)**.
c) The **(calander, calendar)** contains twelve months.

539

34

a) f

b) ph

Spelling by Sound

trash   sherbet   gashes

a) What one sound is created by two letters in each word?

b) What are the letters which represent this sound?

13

Verb Suffixes

conference or **conferance?**

Confer is a verb. It ends in a vowel plus an **r.** The accent is on the last syllable. The correct form is therefore **(conference, conferance).**

72

arrangeable

Final Silent E after Soft C or G

serviceable or **servicable?**

Service ends with a soft **c** followed by a silent **e.** The suffix **-able** begins with an **a.** The correct spelling is therefore ....

131

One-Syllable Adjectives Ending in Y

sly plus **-ly**=**slyly**   **dry** plus **ly**=**dryly**

The word **sly** and the word **dry** are one-syllable words. Each of them is an adjective (a word used to modify a noun). Keep the **y** before adding **-ly** or **-ness.** The correct forms are **(slyly, slily)** and **(dryness, driness).**

190

Doubling the Final Consonant

Select the correct word:

a) The teacher **(demurred, demured)** when asked to chaperone the dance.

b) She stated that she had long **(refrained, refrainned)** from attending evening activities.

c) We felt it unfortunate that she should be **(chainned, chained)** to her home in this way.

249

35

	NOUNS ENDING IN O
a) children	**tomatos** or **tomatoes?**
b) feet	**Rule:** Some nouns ending in **o** form the plural by adding **-es.** There are four common ones that you should know.
c) geese	
d) oxen	tomato potato halo domino
e) lice	Which is correct, **tomatos** or **tomatoes?**
	308

When CH Sounds Like K

a) chorus
b) chromatic
c) characteristic
d) cholesterol

Which word in each group does **not** contain a **k** sound?

a) **choral   chorus   chemical   cheep**
b) **chromium   chest   chronicler   psychologist**
c) **cholera   chlorine   chuckle   chrysanthemum**
d) **chasm   chase   chloroform   chaos**
e) **chronic   hypochondria   charted   technique**   **366**

The Silent T

a) silent
b) sounded

mortgage

A **mortgage** is a matter of special concern to anyone whose property is saddled with one. The sound of the word is also special, for its **t** is silent. Probably the reason is that the **t** in the original French word **mort** (the root of **mortgage**) is silent.

424

Homonyms

a) Its

its

b) It's

led and **lead**

Led is the past form of the verb "to lead." **Lead** is a heavy metal. It is also the common name for the form of carbon (graphite) used in pencils.

482

Select the correct spellings.

a) campaign
b) bookkeeper
c) calendar

cellophane   complexion   cordially   embarrass
a) He had a sallow (**complection, complexion**).
b) He greeted me (**cordially, cordjally**).
c) I found the situation most (**embarasing, embarassing, embarrassing**).
d) The candy is packed in (**celophane, sellophane, sellofane, cellophane**).   **540**

Spelling by Sound

a) sh

b) s, h

teeth think width

a) What one sound is created by two letters in each word?

b) What are the letters which represent this sound?

14

Verb Suffixes

conference

A verb root ending in a vowel plus an **r,** with the accent on its last syllable, takes the suffixes **-ence** and **-ent.** The verb roots are thus changed to nouns.

Change each of the following verbs to nouns:

a) **refer** becomes..........   *c*) **defer** becomes..........

b) **prefer** becomes.........   *d*) **infer** becomes **73**

---

serviceable

a) Something which gives you an advantage is **(advantageous, advantagous).**

b) If you can see something, then it is **(noticable, noticeable).**

c) The moods of young people are very **(changable, changeable).**

d) The prime minister has **(peacable, peaceable)** intentions. **132**

---

slyly

dryness

Keep the **y** before adding **-ly** or **-ness.**

a) The word **sly** is a one-syllable adjective ending in a consonant followed by a **y.** When you add the **-ness** suffix, the correct spelling is **(slyness, sliness).**

b) The word **dry** is another one-syllable adjective which follows the same rule. The correct spelling is therefore **(driness, dryness).** **191**

---

a) demurred

b) refrained

c) chained

Select the correct word:

a) Why am I **(compeled, compelled)** to sit in this chair?

b) How many members are there on your social **(committee, commitee)?**

c) The butler smiled and **(admitted, admited)** us.

d) I have **(submited, submitted)** to your domination for long enough! **250**

37

tomatoes

Nouns Ending in O

Select the correct word:

a) Will you join me in a game of **(dominos, dominoes)**?

b) The staple food of the Irish farmers of the last century was **(potatos, potatoes)**.

309

---

a) cheep

b) chest

c) chuckle

d) chase

e) charted

ALTERNATE SOUNDS OF C

The two common sounds of **c**—**s** and **k**.

The sound of the letter **c** depends upon the letter which follows the **c**. The rule is simple:

Rule: **C** has the sound of **s** when it is followed by **e, i,** or **y**. **C** has the sound of **k** when followed by any other letter.

367

THE SILENT H

Watch your **rhythm**.

The letter **h** is silent when it follows **r** at the beginning of a word. Thus, the **h** is silent in **rhythm**. The **rh** combination appears in some important place names, including **Rhine, Rhodesia, Rheims, Rhode Island** and **Rhodes**. In each case, the **h** is **(silent, sounded)**.

425

Homonyms

led and **lead**

Select the correct word:

a) Recently I visited some **(lead, led)** mines.

b) He **(led, lead)** me to the **(led, lead)** pencil factory.

c) The toys were heavily **(ledded, leaded)**.

483

---

a) complexion

b) cordially

c) embarrassing

d) cellophane

Select the correct spellings.

desperate   extraordinary   government   familiar

a) Suddenly I was **(desparate, despirate, desperate)**.

b) The weather was **(exterordinary, extrordinary, extraordinary)**.

c) He works for the **(goverment, govement, government)**.

d) Your face is **(familyar, familiar)**.

541

Spelling by Sound

a) th

b) t, h

To sum up:

Rule 1: Usually each sound is represented by a written letter, but sometimes—

a) One letter can represent two sounds (x).

b) Or two letters must be used for one sound (sh, th, ph).

15

Verb Suffixes

a) reference

b) preference

c) deference

d) inference

A noun made from a verb root usually means "the act of (whatever the verb means)." **Preference** means the act of preferring. **Reference** means the act of referring.

What does **interference** mean? It is the act of.........

What does **transference** mean? It is the act of.........

74

Final Silent E Before a Suffix

a) advantageous

b) noticeable

c) changeable

d) peaceable

a) He was now face to face with a most **(couragous, courageous)** opponent.

b) You are **(absolutly, absolutely)** correct, my friend.

c) The **(ungrateful, ungratful)** beast was guilty of an **(outragous, outrageous)** attack upon its master.

133

One-Syllable Adjectives Ending in Y

a) slyness

b) dryness

a) The adjective **wry** means "twisted," and is usually used to refer to the appearance of your face when you smile **(wrily, wryly)**.

b) The little girl mounted the platform and looked **(shily, shyly)** at the audience.

c) Her parents failed to understand the reason for her **(shyness, shiness)**.

192

a) compelled

b) committee

c) admitted

d) submitted

Select the correct word:

a) Your letter has been **(referred, refered)** to the appropriate office for prompt action.

b) He could not be **(detered, deterred)** from his evil plan.

c) Thank you for **(remiting, remitting)** payment so promptly.

d) The ship is being **(refited, refitted)** in this yard.

251

Nouns Ending in O

a) dominoes

b) potatoes

rodeos or rodeoes?   pianos or pianoes?
A double rule: A. If a noun ends in a vowel followed by an **o**, form the plural by adding **s**.
B. Any noun ending in **o** that refers to music forms its plural by adding **s**.
The correct forms are **(rodeos, rodeoes)** and **(pianos, pianoes)**.   310

Alternate Sounds of C

What are the six words which contain the **k** sound of **c**?

civilian	bicycle	diced	uncommon
castaway	receive	lacy	celery
cents	scene	perceive	traced
recite	icecap	saccharine	circular 368

The Silent H
More **rh** words.

silent

Here are the more common words beginning with a silent **h** in the **rh** combination; check meanings in your dictionary.

rhapsody	rhetoric	rhinestone	rhubarb
rheostat	rheumatic	rhinoceros	rhyme
rhesus	rheumatism	rhombus	rhythm 426

a) lead

b) led

lead

c) leaded

moral and **morale** (not homonyms if pronounced correctly).
Moral is used as an adjective to indicate ethical conduct or attitude, or as the lesson of a story. **Morale** is used to indicate enthusiasm or a good sense of cooperation. The accent is on the first syllable of **moral,** on the second of **morale.**   484

a) desperate

b) extraordinary

c) government

d) familiar

Cover the centered words before doing the questions. Select the correct spellings.
            exaggerate fatigue grocery ninety
a) Please do not (eggsagerate, exaggerate, exajerate).
b) The great effort caused (fetigue, fatigue, fateeg).
c) This shop is a (grosery, groccry, grocerey).
d) He counted up to (ninty, ninety).   542

40

Spelling by Sound

Here is another rule:

Rule 2: When you spell a word, write the letters in the same order in which you hear them.

a) In **clams,** what is the order of m and s?

b) In **chasm,** what is the order of m and s?

16

ADJECTIVE SUFFIXES

interfering

transferring

An adjective is a word used to modify a noun. Many adjectives meaning "capable" or "able to" end in **-able** or **-ible.**

The -able Rule: If the noun from which the adjective is formed ends with **-ation,** the adjective suffix will be **-able.**

75

Final Silent E Before a Suffix

a) courageous

b) absolutely

c) ungrateful

  outrageous

a) The loss was directly **(traceable, tracable)** to the **(carless, careless)** workers.

b) He was **(noticably, noticeably)** upset by your words.

c) It would be **(incredable, incredible)** to hear that an automobile as old as yours is still considered **(garagable, garageable).**

134

a) wryly

b) shyly

c) shyness

a) I cannot understand what you are **(triing, trying)** to do.

b) The **(sliness, slyness)** of the fox is legendary.

c) The **(dryness, driness)** of the air will help you.

d) How **(sprily, spryly)** the old man danced!

e) His **(spryness, spriness)** surprised everyone.

f) I should have understood when he smiled **(slyly, slily).**

193

Doubling the Final Consonant

a) referred

b) deterred

c) remitting

d) refitted

Correct the three misspelled words.

Henry has **sprained** his ankle. The accident **occured** on the day that he **committed** a serious error. The mayor has **offered** him a **commitee** membership. Henry became so overjoyed that he **butted** his head against a beam while rushing home. The **accidenttal** fall has put him to bed.

252

41

Nouns Ending in O

Select the correct word:

rodeos

pianos

a) The work is one of the few written for four **(pianos, pianoes)**.
b) Everyone in the audience was thrilled by the excellence of her **(soloes, solos)**.
c) Mary and Jane are our most competent **(altos, altoes)**.

311

Alternate Sounds of C

castaway
bicycle
icecap
saccharine
uncommon
circular

Write the six words which contain the **s** sound of **c**.

precise	climbing	cosine
tack	succeed	clocks
choral	talcum	pincers
psychology	technical	cyclical
patience	decently	cobalt

369

REVIEW (X)

a) The letter **c** has the sound **s** when it is followed by (a vowel, the letter **t**, the letter **e**).
b) The word in which the **c** has the sound **s** is:

tracks   scanning   recess   cubes

c) The sound of **c** in patience is **(k, s, sh)**.

427

---

moral and morale

Select the correct word:

a) The soldiers display good **(moral, morale)**.
b) Moses gave the world a lasting **(moral, morale)**.
c) The general is a man of high **(morals, morales)**.
d) The bishop preached about **(morality, moraleity)**.

485

Cover the centered words before doing the questions.
Select the correct spellings.

a) exaggerate

b) fatigue

c) grocery

d) ninety

interrupt   immense   magazine   sanitary

a) Please do not **(interupt, intarupt, interrupt)**.
b) The giant was **(amense, imense, immense)**.
c) He writes for a famous **(magezine, magazeen, magazine)**.
d) They enforce the **(sanatary, sanitary)** laws.

543

42

Spelling by Sound

Now let us have another look at long and short vowels. In each of these groups of words are the vowels long or short?

a) **catch**	**pat**	**sack**
b) **finish**	**lit**	**mill**
c) **cot**	**lob**	**rock**

17

Adjective Suffixes

admirable or **admirible**?

The related noun is **admiration**. This word ends in **-ation**. The **-able** rule is followed.

The correct form is therefore **(admirable, admirible)**.

76

---

a) traceable

careless

b) noticeably

c) incredible

garageable

Final Silent E after U or W

truely or **truly**?

Exception to the rule in Frame 122: Drop the final silent **e** after the letters **u** or **w,** and then add your suffix.

In **true,** the final **e** is preceded by a **u.** Therefore, the final **e** is dropped, giving the word **(truly, truely).**

135

---

a) trying
b) slyness
c) dryness
d) spryly
e) spryness
f) slyly

REVIEW (V)

a) When you add a suffix beginning with a consonant to the word **complete,** you (keep, drop) the final **e.**

b) The combination of the word **involve** and the suffix **-ment** is the new word **(involvment, involvement).**

194

---

occurred

committee

accidental

WORDS ENDING IN DOUBLE CONSONANT

enchanted or **enchantted? conference** or **conference?**

Rule: Do not double the final consonant when the word has more than one syllable, and ends in a double consonant.

253

Irregular Plurals

Is the plural of **deer** (**deer** or **deers**)?
A group of exceptions: Some nouns are the same in the singular as in the plural. These fall into two groups: The first includes certain animals, such as **deer, sheep,** or the fish called **trout, mackerel, halibut,** and many others.

a) pianos
b) solos
c) altos

312

Sometimes the **c** sounds like **sh**.
There is a small number of words in which **c** followed by an **i** or an **e** has the sound **sh**. Among the most common of these are:

ocean	**tenacious**	**efficient**	**precocious**
suspicion	**deficient**	**ferocious**	**vicious**
precious	**Fascist**	**conscience**	**official**
facial	**racial**	**conscious**	**sufficient**

precise
patience
succeed
decently
pincers
cyclical

370

Review (X)

a) Which word does **not** have the sound **sh** for **c**?
    transoceanic   conscious   officially   officer
b) Which of these words has the sound **sh** for **c**?
        paces   cast   Fascist   precocity
c) The sound of **sc** in **descending** is (**sk, k, s**).

a) the letter e
b) recess
c) s

428

---

passed and **past**

Passed is the past form of the verb "to pass." **Past** is used as a noun (the **past** is not forgotten); as an adjective (the **past** year was busy); and as a preposition to indicate motion or position beyond a specified point.
I (**passed, past**) your home when I drove (**passed, past**) the street in which my (**passed, past**) began.

a) morale
b) moral
c) morals
d) morality

486

Cover the centered words before doing the questions. Select the correct spellings.
        valuable   opposite   occasion   similar
a) The jewels are (**valuble, valyuble, valuable**).
b) His room is (**opazit, opposit, opposite**) mine.
c) It was a joyous (**ocasion, occasion**).
d) The symptoms were (**simalar, simillar, similar**).

a) interrupt
b) immense
c) magazine
d) sanitary

544

44

a) short
b) short
c) short

Spelling by Sound

Some vowels in the following words must be short, because we do not say them the way we say the vowels in alphabetical order.

Which two words below have only short vowels?

fin   fine   rate   cat   bone

18

-able or **-ible**? (Use **-able** if the root noun ends in **-ation**).

admirable

a) The adjective formed from **demonstration** is
....

b) From **imagination** we get..................

c) ....is formed from **duration.**

d) A river on which **navigation** is possible is called a .... river. **77**

---

truly

FINAL SILENT E AFTER U OR W
aweful or awful?

The root word is **awe**. Note that it ends in a **w** followed by a silent **e**. Our rule is that you drop the final **e** after the letter **w**. The correct word is therefore (**aweful, awful**).

136

Review (V)

a) keep

b) involvement

Find and correct the three misspelled words.

I have always found her actions admirable. She has never been guilty of refuseing to assist those who needed assistence. But I was greatly dissatisfied to hear of her carelessness and the resultant fire in her basment.

195

Doubling the Final Consonant
enchanted or enchantted?

The word **enchant** is a two-syllable word. It ends in a double consonant. In other forms, then, **enchant** does not double its final letter.

The correct spelling is therefore (**enchanted, enchantted**).

254

Irregular Plurals

The other exceptions: The name applied to the people of a country when that name ends in **-ese** is usually the same for the singular and the plural. Thus, one man is a Japanese, and ten Japanese people are spoken of as ten **(Japanese, Japaneses).**

313

Alternate Sounds of C

Each of the words below has the sound **sh** in it, but some of them have been spelled with the **sh** where they should have a **c.** Correct these words. There are six of them.

cashing	splashing	unabashed
vishious	osheanic	effishiency
conshious	Fashist	precoshious

371

Review (X)

Select the correct answer.
a) The soldiers were called **(lansers, lancers).**
b) In the word **insignia** the **g** is **(silent, sounded).**
c) In the word **ignoble** the **g** is **(sounded, silent).**

a) officer
b) Fascist
c) s

429

Homonyms

plain and plane

Plain means clear or easy to understand as well as the opposite of **handsome** or **pretty.** It also is the name for a flat area of land. A third meaning is as in **plain** view, meaning free of obstacles.
A **plane** is a level space as well as a tool used in carpentry.

passed

past

past

487

FINAL REVIEW (XII)

Correct the **misspelled** word in each group.
a) **submersible siezing climbing passable**
b) **patiently interference subtly stired**
c) **allways exceed deficit amateur**
d) **appetite confered lapsed technique**

a) valuable
b) opposite
c) occasion
d) similar

545

Spelling by Sound

fin

cat

The short vowels in **fin** and **cat** were **short i** and **short a**. Other short vowels are:
Short **e**: as in **rest, pet**, and **wren**
Short **u**: as in **cut, fun**, and **rust**
Short **y**: as in **crypt** and **typical**
What is the short vowel in **return?**

19

Adjective Suffixes

a) demonstrable

b) imaginable

c) durable

d) navigable

reducible or **reducable?**
The -ible Rule: If the root noun from which the adjective is formed ends in **-tion, -sion, -ition** (but **not -ation**), the suffix will be **-ible.**
The root noun is **reduction.** Is the adjective **reducible** or **reducable?**

78

Final Silent E after U or W

awful

a) Which is correct, **duely** or **duly?**
b) Do people have **arguements** or **arguments?**
c) Did he speak **untruly** or **untruely?**

137

Review (V)

refusing

assistance

basement

a) Why do you think he acted so **(courageously, couragously)?**
b) Is the needle **(replacable, replaceable)?**
c) I have been **(tracing, traceing)** his actions.
d) The **(rearrangement, rearrangment)** of the furniture required the rest of the working day.

196

Doubling the Final Consonant

enchanted

conferrence or **conference?**
Rule: Do not double the final consonant when the accent shifts from the last syllable when an ending beginning with a vowel is added, even though the word ends with a single vowel followed by a consonant.

255

47

Irregular Plurals

Select the correct word:
a) I saw many **(beaver, beavers)** working on the dam.
b) How many **(sheep, sheeps)** does the farmer own?
c) I saw a group of **(wolf, wolves)** in the zoo.
d) We caught many **(herring, herrings)** last week.

314

---

vicious
conscious
oceanic
Fascist
efficiency
precocious

Alternate Sounds of C

c and s in the same word—**incense**
Many words which contain both a **c** and an **s**
have the sound of **s** twice.
a) The sound of **c** in **license** is **(s, k)**.
b) The sound of **c** in **scenery** is **(s, k)**.
c) What is the sound of the **c** in **census**?

372

---

a) lancers

b) sounded

c) sounded

Review (X)

a) There is a silent **g** in **(signify, dignity, designing)**.
b) The interval between two rulers, when a country
has no sovereign, is called the **interregnum**. The **g**
in the word is **(silent, sounded)**.
c) An occasional vacation is considered **(sensible, sencible)**.

430

Homonyms

Select the correct word:
His **(plane, plain)** features were filled with joy as his
motorboat **(plained, planed)** over the water. He had
been raised on the flatlands of his native **(plain, plane)**, and had never known the pleasure he now
experienced for the first time.

488

---

a) seizing

b) stirred

c) always

d) conferred

Review (XII)

Correct the five **misspelled** or **incorrectly used** words
in the paragraph.
The disease may break out without warning. Its
wierd symptoms baffle doctors, and few patience
succeed in escaping its affects. It is curible only if
caught during its first hours. Last year, a town was
wholly wiped out by this plague.

546

short u

Spelling by Sound

From the words below:

a) Select the three words with short vowels only.

b) Select the words with one long vowel.

repent   pure   step   trip   slant

20

---

reducible

Adjective Suffixes

a) The root noun is **corruption.** Is the related adjective **corruptable** or **corruptible?**

b) Which is correct, **collectible** or **collectable?**

c) What is the related word which helped you decide the correct answer to question *b)* above?

79

---

a) duly

b) arguments

c) untruly

Final Silent E after U or W

a) The villain was acting in a **(roguish, rogueish)** manner.

b) The child was **(plagueing, plaguing)** me with his repeated demands for sweets.

c) **(Oweing, owing)** money to a friend is sometimes foolish.

138

---

a) courageously

b) replaceable

c) tracing

d) rearrange-
     ment

Review (V)

a) He is an **(unruly, unruely)** child.

b) Why are you **(plagueing, plaguing)** him so?

c) You and the others speak **(untruly, untruely).**

d) Your essay is a masterpiece of **(vaguness, vagueness).**

e) When I saw them they were **(argucing, arguing).**

197

Doubling the Final Consonant

conferrence or conference?

Remember the rule: The final consonant is **not** doubled when the accent shifts from the last syllable.

Since the accent shifts, the correct spelling is **(conferrence, conference).**

256

Irregular Plurals

a) beavers

b) sheep

c) wolves

d) herring

Select the correct word:
a) Did you know he bought tons of **(tuna, tunas)**?
b) They are all **(Englishman, Englishmen)**.
c) The theatre group contains six **(Chinese, Chineses)**.
d) The cats are called **(Siamese, Siameses)**.

315

Alternate Sounds of C

a) s

b) s

c) s

Select the correct spelling:
a) The water was found at the **(oacis, oasis)**.
b) Please turn off the **(fauset, faucet)**.
c) The rider tightened the **(sinch, cinch)**.
d) I would like this noise to **(sease, cease)**.
e) They were overjoyed when they opened the **(parsel, parcel)**.

373

Review (X)

a) designing

b) sounded

c) sensible

a) Is the correct spelling **exsede, exceed,** or **exseed**?
b) The plural of knife is **(knifes, knives)**.
c) The correct spelling is **(knowladge, knowledge, knowlidge)**.

431

Homonyms

plain

planed

plain

Select the correct word:
a) He is **(all together, altogether)** evil.
b) Genghis Khan **(lead, led)** his hordes across the mountains, trusting to their high **(moral, morale)** to keep them together until they reached the **(plain, plane)**.

489

Review (XII)

weird

patients

effects

curable

wholly

Which word in each group has a silent letter or letters?
a) spasm   cycling   impugn   sparkler
b) pauper   honey   limber   limb
c) wedded   redwing   castles   receding
d) vowel   misspell   designate   designer

547

a) step

trip

slant

b) repent

pure

Spelling by Sound

As we saw, the long **o** has the sound of the name of the letter, as in **over.** The sound of o (as in **cot**) is a short **o.**

Write the three words in the group below that have a short **o.**

   token   opening   lot   on   crony   possible

21

---

a) corruptible

b) collectible

c) collection

Adjective Suffixes

a) Is something which is easily changed **convertable** or **convertible?**

b) What related word helped you decide *a*) above?

c) Is something which you admit **admissible** or **admissable?**

d) What is the related word in *c*) above?

e) Think back! Is it **admirible** or **admirable?**   80

---

a) roguish

b) plaguing

c) owing

Find and correct the four misspelled words.

Your letter was **duely** received, and I hasten to refute your **arguements.** What **aweful** motive could cause this **plaguing** of a friend? You know I am not guilty of **harangueing** the other club members. I am most **truly** sorry that you could have thought I was.

139

---

a) unruly

b) plaguing

c) untruly

d) vagueness

e) arguing

Review (V)

Here is a list of words ending in **-ieing** or **-ying.** Correct the four words which have been misspelled.

   dying   paying   replieing

   frying   vieing   defieing

   tying   lieing   trying

198

---

conference

Select the correct word:

a) It is good to see that you are at last **(repenttant, repentant).**

b) Will you supply me with a better **(reference, referrence)?**

c) I will make the **(referal, referral)** you requested.

d) This antiseptic will prevent any **(infecttion, infection).**   257

51

Noun Plurals

Select the correct word:

a) tuna

b) Englishmen

c) Chinese

d) Siamese

a) Napoleon saw three troops of **(German, Germans)**.

b) The women were **(Burmeses, Burmese)**.

c) Good restaurants require good **(chefes, chefs)**.

d) The bathing beauty was noted for her shapely **(calfs, calves)**. 316

Alternate Sounds of C

Select the correct spelling. These are more difficult than the words in Frame 373.

a) oasis

b) faucet

c) cinch

d) cease

e) parcel

a) All **(cigns, signs)** lead to the shuttle train.

b) I learned to respect my **(ancestors, anscestors)**.

c) The house was made of **(sinder, cinder)** blocks.

d) Enough of your **(suspishions, suspicions)**.

e) No man can **(supersede, supercede)** the king. 374

Review (X)

a) exceed

b) knives

c) knowledge

a) The two-syllable word for a form of soft coal is **lignite,** rhyming with **night.** The g is **(silent, sounded)**.

b) The g in the word **significant** is **(silent, sounded)**.

c) The sound of g in the word **gnu** is **(silent, pronounced)**.

d) When you pretend, you are **(feigning, fiegning)**. 432

Homonyms

Select the correct word:

a) altogether

b) led

morale

plain

a) Some doctors praise the value of **(coarse, course)** foods.

b) **(It's, Its)** time for the group to hold **(it's, its)** annual festival and dance.

c) His **(passed, past)** experience with guns explains why he **(passed, past)** the **(coarse, course)**. 490

Review (XII)

a) impugn

b) limb

c) castles

d) designer

Correct the **misspelled** word in each group.

a) **sanitary   athelete   village   February**

b) **usually   finally   capitel   disappoint**

c) **necessity   problem   celary   hygiene**

d) **untyed   promise   chasm   procession**

548

lot
on
possible

Spelling by Sound
Notice the letter **e** in the following words:
note fine race core
In each word, is it pronounced or silent?

22

a) convertible

b) conversion

c) admissible

d) admission

e) admirable

Adjective Suffixes
Detestable comes from the word **detest.**
Eatable comes from the word **eat.**
Excitable comes from the word **excite.**
Another -able Rule: If the root word is a full word, or a full word with its final **e** removed, then the suffix is usually **-able.**

81

a) duly

b) arguments

c) awful

d) haranguing

Final Silent E after U or W
vaguely or vaguly?
An exception to our exception: You have been warned that the English language is filled with exceptions to the rules of spelling. The word **vague** is one of these. Keep the final **e**, which gives you **(vaguely, vaguly)** and **(vagueness, vaguness).**

140

vying

lying

replying

defying

Review (V)
a) Which is correct, **eyeing** or **eying?**
b) Every golfer learns to understand the importance of correct **(teing, teeing).**
c) The wrestler was accused of deliberate **(kneeing, kneing).**
d) It was Abraham Lincoln who was best remembered for success in **(freing, freeing)** slaves.

199

a) repentant

b) reference

c) referral

d) infection

Doubling the Final Consonant
Select the correct word:
a) He has **(returned, returnned)** from the party.
b) The waters seem strangely **(unsetled, unsettled).**
c) For what reason must the tooth be **(extractted, extracted)?**
d) The dentist tells us that it is badly **(infectted, infected).**

258

53

Noun Plurals

a) Germans

b) Burmese

c) chefs

d) calves

Select the correct word:

a) The ice particles stung like (knifes, **knives**).

b) This is the saloon reserved for (ladys, **ladies**).

c) I was able to catch three large (**trout**, trouts).

d) The traders who brought goods from Asia to France were a group of clever (Malteses, **Maltese**).

317

Alternate Sounds of C

a) signs

b) ancestors

c) cinder

d) suspicions

e) supersede

Select the correct spelling:

a) These laws were intended to abate (nuisanses, **nuisances**).

b) He was threatened with the loss of his (**licence**, license).

c) Why is that dog so (visious, **vicious**)?

d) The blow left him (unconsious, **unconscious**).

375

Review (X)

a) sounded

b) sounded

c) silent

d) feigning

a) How many silent first letters are there in the sentence: **I knew the gnu was new to the zoo.**

b) The Book of (Salms, **Psalms**) is ascribed to David.

c) The word containing a silent **p** is:

premier   ptomaine   lapse   imps

433

Homonyms

a) coarse

b) It's

its

c) past

passed

course

principal and **principle**

Principal refers to an authority or chief person, or main thing; to the one who takes the lead; and sometimes to a fundamental point.

Principle refers to a rule of conduct or to a belief.

The (**principal**, principle) of gravity explains why the (principal, **principle**) fell down.

491

Review (XII)

a) athlete

b) capital or capitol

c) celery

d) untied

a) Every syllable must have at least one (**vowel**, consonant).

b) How many words end in -sede?

c) If you **inter** someone, he has been (intered, **interred**).

d) His face was suddenly (radient, **radiant**).

549

54

Spelling by Sound

silent

The **e** in each of these words **(note, fine, race, core)** is silent, but it has made the preceding vowel in each word long.
Which of the initial vowels in these words are long?

sigh   **these**   **made**   **day**

23

Adjective Suffixes

a) From the word **size** we get **(sizable, sizible)**.
b) Is it **laughible** or **laughable?**
c) The root word in *b)* above is ....

82

FINAL IE BEFORE -ING

vaguely

vagueness

lieing or **lying?**   **dieing** or **dying?**
Another exception—a rule in itself:
When a word ends in **ie,** change the letters **ie** to a **y** before adding **-ing.**

141

a) eyeing

b) teeing

c) kneeing

d) freeing

Review (V)

a) Which is correct, **enjoying** or **enjoing?**
b) The army was **(deploied, deployed)** on the hilltop.
c) The healthiest people in our country live in our northern **(vallies, valleys).**
d) What are you **(saing, saying)?**

200

a) returned

b) unsettled

c) extracted

d) infected

Doubling the Final Consonant

Select the correct word:
a) What a **(marvelous, marvellous)** painting this is!
b) Yes, it is a **(remarkkable, remarkable)** likeness.
c) How much are you **(deducting, deductting)** from the price?
d) He knows what to do when **(subtracting, subtractting).**

259

55

Noun Plurals

a) knives

b) ladies

c) trout

d) Maltese

Select the correct word:

a) The candidates made several (speechs, speeches).

b) He drank large (quantities, quantitys) of wine.

c) The orphanage was filled with homeless (waifs, waives).

318

Alternate Sounds of C

a) nuisances

b) license

c) vicious

d) unconscious

Correct the misspelled word in each group.

a) circular   ensircle   ceasing   receded

b) anscestry   ancestors   scented   ascending

c) precisely   precicion   decisive   contrary

d) deduce   introduce   produser   user

e) parsel   farcical   racist   passion

376

Review (X)

a) 2 (k and g)

b) Psalms

c) ptomaine

a) Most words beginning with wr have a meaning related to (fighting, twisting, pulling).

b) When you argue, you may be (wreathing, wrangling).

c) How many silent letters are there in wrought?

434

Homonyms

Select the correct word:

principle

principal

a) What are the (principal, principle) reasons for your success on this job?

b) He is a man of high (principals, principles), (which, witch) explains his decision.

c) He is one of the (principals, principles) of the firm.

492

Review (XII)

a) vowel

b) l

c) interred

d) radiant

a) The tiger was snarling and (spitting, spiting).

b) This is a happy (ocasion, occasion).

c) His house faces the old (cemetery, cemetary).

d) Is my application (admissable, admissible)?

e) The (preist, priest) is (praying, praeing).

550

all of them

Spelling by Sound
In the words below, two letters are used to give the sound of a single letter.

day   paid   neigh   convey

What letters give the sound of long **a**?

24

a) sizable

b) laughable

c) laugh

Adjective Suffixes
a) Someone upon whom you can depend is **(dependible, dependable)**.
b) Someone people admire is **(admirable, admirible)**.
c) Something which assists your comprehension is **(comprehensible, comprehensable)**.

83

Final IE before -ING
lieing or **lying?**
The word **lie** ends in **ie**. That means that it follows our rule. To add **-ing**, you first change the ending **-ie** to a **y**. The correct spelling is thus **(lieing, lying)**.

142

a) enjoying

b) deployed

c) valleys

d) saying

Review (V)
a) The **(unreadyness, unreadiness)** of the defenders gave an easy victory to Morgan's forces.
b) Are you **(relying, reliing)** on his promise?
c) Oh, what a **(beautiful, beautyful)** day!
d) What sort of **(business, busyness)** are you in?

201

a) marvelous

b) remarkable

c) deducting

d) subtracting

Select the correct word:
a) He could not understand why she **(braged, bragged)**.
b) There is great popular **(preference, preferrence)** for beer.
c) I respect those men who bravely **(steped, stepped)** forward.
d) Which is correct, **happenned** or **happened**?

260

57

Noun Plurals

a) speeches

b) quantities

c) waifs

Select the correct word:
a) The old town was a maze of narrow **(alleyes, alleys)**.
b) The computer was activated by its **(relays, relayes)**.
c) All of the workmen were **(Japanese, Japaneses)**.

319

---

a) encircle

b) ancestry

c) precision

d) producer

e) parcel

ENDINGS IN -ERY AND -ARY

secretary or **secretery**? **cemetery** or **cemetary**?
This pair of words has long bewildered students of spelling. It is the ending which creates confusion. Try these sentences as memory aids:
a) A good **secretary** does not **tarry**. SECRETARY.
b) **Jerry** works at the **cemetery**. CEMETERY.

377

---

a) twisting

b) wrangling

c) 3

Review (X)

a) The **sh** sound of **c** is found in **(vivacious, vivacity)**.
b) The adjective **ancillary** means additional, or helping. Its **c** sound is **(k, sh, s)**.
c) **Decade** has the same **c** sound as **(cents, cones, city)**.
d) The word with a silent letter is **(tower, wrestle)**.

435

---

a) principal

b) principles

which

c) principals

Homonyms

shone and **shown**

Shone is the past form of the verb "to shine."
Shown is the past form of "to show," meaning "revealed."

493

---

a) spitting

b) occasion

c) cemetery

d) admissible

e) priest

praying

Review (XII)

Correct the five **misspelled** words:
The oldest man I know is a foriegner who arrived from his native land half a century ago. He failled to aply for citizenship, and it has not been posible for him to vote. However, he loves his adopted land.

551

Spelling by Sound
In the words below, two letters are used to give the sound of long **e**.

cheese   leap   piece   seize

Which of the words below also contain long vowel sounds?

sleigh   fade   carp   please   chief   25

---

a) dependable

b) admirable

c) comprehensible

a) The word **movable** comes from the root word ....

b) From **rotation** we get (**rotatible, rotatable**).

c) Which is correct, **desirable** or **desirible**?

d) Something which you can **credit** as true is (**creditible, creditable**).

e) If you can **market** it, it is (**marketable, marketible**).   84

---

lying

Final IE before -ING
dieing or **dying**?

Remember the rule: When the word ends in **ie**, change the final **ie** to **y** and then add **-ing**.

The word **die** ends in **ie**. Following the rule, the final **ie** becomes a **y**, and the correct spelling is (**dieing, dying**).   143

---

a) unreadiness

b) relying

c) beautiful

d) business

Review (V)
Correct the three misspelled words:

He is a studyous lad whose father is always worrying about him. It was only because he was compliing with his father's demand for perfection that he made his fatal error. He was so anxious to succeed that he copyed someone else's work during an examination.   202

---

a) bragged

b) preference

c) stepped

d) happened

Doubling the Final Consonant
Select the correct word:

a) The wind was of an (**alarming, alarmming**) force.

b) It was I who (**benefited, benefitted**) from the sale.

c) He quickly (**abstractted, abstracted**) the document.

d) The business was most (**profitable, profittable**).   261

Noun Plurals

a) alleys

b) relays

c) Japanese

Here is a list of 12 plurals. Correct the four which are incorrect.

houses	radios	guesses
mouses	tomatos	thieves
louses	altos	beliefs
sopranos	haloes	halibuts

320

Silent Consonants

knife reign sovereign foreign deign

a) He was born in the .... of George V.

b) Louis XVI was an unpopular ....

c) The immigrant came from a .... land.

d) He cut the cord with a ....

e) The proud woman would not .... to answer.

378

a) vivacious

b) s

c) cones

d) wrestle

Review (X)

a) Which of these words has the silent b?
   numbers   crumble   crumbs   tumbler

b) Which of these words has the sounded b?
   dumber   thumbs   combing   stumble

c) The letter b is heard in (clamber, tombs).

436

Homonyms

Select the correct word:

a) The burning sun (shown, shone) down upon the arid (plain, plane).

b) It has been (shown, shone) that exercise will prevent certain muscle ailments.

494

foreigner

failed

apply

possible

adopted

Review (XII)

Correct the 5 misspelled or incorrectly used words:
Our whether has been changeing in recent decades. This is caused niether bye wind currents nor by a change in ocean currents. It is probably a result of the cycles of polar heat which are centurys old.

552

sleigh

fade

please

chief

Spelling by Sound

Here are other ways long vowels are spelled:

Long **i**: seismograph   sigh   lie

Long **o**: grow   load   oh

Select the words below with long vowel sounds:

foal   night   bone   enter

26

---

a) move

b) rotatable

c) desirable

d) creditable

e) marketable

Adjective Suffixes

terrable or **terrible?**

More about -ible: Use the -ible ending for words in which the root is not a recognizable full word. **Terrible** comes from the word **terror.** Since the whole word is not used in making the adjective, you use the **-ible** ending.

Which is correct, **possable** or **possible?**   85

---

dying

Final IE before -ING

a) Scouts who learned how to **tie** ropes carefully and well received an award for **(rope-tying, rope-tieing).**

b) "To vie" means to compete. The scouts were **(vieing, vying)** with one another for the awards.

c) The scout who **(tied, tyed)** the best knots thought of his success as he was **(lieing, lying)** in bed later. 144

---

studious

complying

copied

Review (V)

Correct the five misspelled words:

He said the repayment would be his first dayly thought, for no debt was more truely paiable. The mismanaged affairs of the slayn man were left in an unimaginable state of confusion—so much so that a great burden was layed on his family for years to come.   203

---

a) alarming

b) benefited

c) abstracted

d) profitable

Doubling the Final Consonant

Correct the **incorrect** word in each group:

a) **repelled   repelant   repelling   repel**

b) **repeattable   repeated   repeating   repeat**

c) **defecting   defected   defecttion   defect**

d) **prefering   preferred   preference   prefer**

262

61

mice

lice

tomatoes

halibut

Noun Plurals
Correct the three misspelled words.

geese	potatoes	tongues
teeth	butterflies	leafs
calfs	women	amateurs
elves	Japanese	oxes

321

a) reign

b) sovereign

c) foreign

d) knife

e) deign

Silent Consonants
The silent **p** usually appears at the beginning of words. Your memory must be your guide. Fortunately, most of the silent **p** words contain similar elements and therefore they are fairly easy to remember.
a) Is it **numatic** or **pneumatic?**
b) A sacred song is called a ....

379

a) crumbs

b) stumble

c) clamber

Review (X)
a) One who owes money is a **(debtor, debter).**
b) Which of these words has the greatest number of silent letters?
  hymnal   rhyme   solemnly   listening
c) Which is correct, **damnable** or **damnible?**

437

a) shone

plain

b) shown

stationery and **stationary**
The word **stationary** refers to something that stays in a fixed position. **Stationery** refers to writing paper and related materials.
a) Mr. Johnson decided to open a **(stationery, stationary)** shop which would sell several **(weekly, weakly)** publications.
b) The platform was **(stationery, stationary).**

495

weather

changing

neither

by

centuries

Review (XII)
Correct the 4 **misspelled** or **incorrectly used** words: When I came fourth into the sunlight I realized that I had slept through the night. A freindly policeman directed me to my destination, where I found my beautyful hoarse waiting to carry me on to new adventures.

553

foal
 	
night
 	
bone
	Spelling by Sound
	Long u can be spelled in several different ways:
	eu as in feud **ew** as in few
	ue as in due **eau** as in beauty
	Pick out the words with the long **u** sound:
	    imbue **burr** **refute** **beautiful**
	                                               27

possible	**Adjective Suffixes** **Words ending in -ible.** *a*) One fit to be chosen is **(eligable, eligible)**. *b*) Anything you can hear is **(audible, audable)**. *c*) When the first star can be seen it is **(visable, visible)**. 86
a) rope-tying *b*) vying *c*) tied lying	**Final IE before -ING** Were you trapped by the word "tied" in the *c*) sentence of Frame 144? If so, you forgot that a silent **e** is simply dropped before the suffix **-ed** is added. The existence of a special rule about **ie** becoming a **y** before **-ing** doesn't change the other rules you have learned. Think hard! They say the liar **(lied, lyed)**. **145**
daily truly payable slain laid	**Review (V)** *a*) How **(slily, slyly)** he crept along the ground! *b*) The fire was aided by the **(dryness, driness)** of the grass around the burning house. *c*) The wild horses were renowned for their **(shyness, shiness)**. *d*) He hopped along with surprising **(spriness, spryness)**. **204**
a) repellant *b*) repeatable *c*) defection *d*) preferring	**Doubling the Final Consonant** Which sentence contains an error in spelling? Correct it. *a*) The recurrence of the disease was incredible. *b*) How much equippment do these bragging men need? *c*) The deducting was done automatically. *d*) The dancer tripped after he had flipped twice. **263**

REVIEW (VIII)

calves

leaves

oxen

a) The form of **study** ending in **-ous** is...................
b) Adding the ending **-ous** to **courage** makes..........
c) Is it **carrying** or **carrieing?**...................
d) The person who is most late is **(tardyest, tardiest).**
e) The noisy fan was an **(annoiance, annoyance).** 322

---

a) pneumatic

b) psalm

wr—the twisting, squeezing, turning words

Most of the **wr** words seem to contain some reference to twisting or pressing. The common root of many **wr** words is an old Anglo-Saxon word meaning "twist."

wry   wrapper   wrath

a) A covering around something is called a............
b) The most intense anger is called............ 380

---

a) debtor

b) rhyme

c) damnable

Review (X)

a) Which of these words has the sounded **gh?**
    naught   aghast   sighted   wheelwright
b) Expensive perfumes have a **(subtle, suttle)** scent.
c) Which of these words has a silent letter?
    firing   caps   aptly   indebtedness 438

---

a) stationery

  weekly

b) stationary

threw and through

Threw is the past form of the verb "to throw." **Through** means "in the midst of," or "between the parts of"; it is a preposition.

a) The game began when the referee **(threw, through)** the ball down the field and the **(hole, whole)** team ran forward.
b) The ball sailed **(threw, through)** the air. 496

---

forth

friendly

beautiful

horse

Review (XII)

Correct the 5 **misspelled** or **incorrectly used** words: My assistent was waiting at the bookeeper's office. He urged me to hurry, for the preparrations for the annual comittee meeting included my opening speech. How could I brake my promise to those other women who had worked so long? 554

imbue

refute

beautiful

Spelling by Sound

In addition to the long and short vowel sounds, many other sounds are represented by the six vowels. These sounds are neither long nor short, but somewhere in between.

Which of these words contains a vowel which does **not** give either a definite long or short sound?

over   cape   horn   oil   farther   slip   28

---

a) eligible

b) audible

c) visible

Adjective Suffixes

Words ending in -ible.

a) If you can believe a story, it is usually **(plausible, plausable)**.

b) Anything that can happen is **(possable, possible)**.

c) If it causes a feeling of horror, then you speak of something as **(horrible, horrable)**.   87

---

lied

FINAL SILENT E BEFORE -ING

eyeing or **eying**? **hoeing** or **hoing**? **seeing** or **seing**? Another important rule: Keep the silent final **e** before you add **-ing** to words that end in **ye, oe** or **ee**.

146

TIME TO TAKE STOCK

a) slyly

b) dryness

c) shyness

d) spryness

How well have you been doing? You should have achieved a perfect score in Review V. If you did not, then take the time to restudy the groups of frames for which you did not have correct answers. Then, as soon as you are sure you clearly understand all of the previous material, move on to the next frame.   205

REVIEW (VII)

b) equipment

a) With which of these words do you double the final consonant before adding the ending **-ing**?

defer   cap   resist   prevent   slip

b) Which of these words should not end in **-ible**?

possible   regrettible   feasible   illegible

264

a) studious	**Review (VIII)**
b) courageous	What is the missing letter or letters?
	a) Hiroshima was completely destro......d.
c) carrying	*b*) In time, even he will be satisf......d.
	c) I could not hear what you s......d.
d) tardiest	*d*) His hand was never stead......r.
e) annoyance	*e*) His paintings are most fanc......ful.

323

Review of Confusing Sounds

a) wrapper

b) wrath

Select the correct answer:
a) The sound of **ch** in chauffeur is **(k, ch, sh)**.
b) The **g** in **signify** is **(sounded, silent)**.
c) The sound of **c** in **fascination** is **(s, k)**.

381

Review (X)

a) aghast

b) subtle

c) indebtedness

Among the group of words at the bottom of this frame:
a) Which have the silent **gh?**
b) Which have the sound f for **gh?**
c) Which has the hard g sound?
slaughterhouse   toga   coughing   roughly   boughs 439

Homonyms
who's and whose

a) threw

whole

b) through

Who's is the contraction of "who is." **Whose** is a pronoun showing possession.
a) **(Who's, Whose)** the woman **(who's, whose)** flowers won first prize when **(shone, shown)** at the fair?
b) I know **(who's, whose)** book this is.

497

assistant

bookkeeper's

preparations

committee

break

Review (XII)

Correct the **misspelled** word in each group:
a) **ineligible   palatible   incredible   possible**
b) **pleasant   intolerant   apparant   radiant**
c) **manageing   peaceable   courageous   arranged**
d) **hitting   sitting   fitting   assistting**

555

66

over

horn

oil

farther

Spelling by Sound

Pronounce these words. Listen carefully to the sounds of the designated letters:

dollar   parity   faces   analysis   rarefy

Do you hear these sounds?

29

---

a) plausible

b) possible

c) horrible

Practice with -able and -ible.

a) An army that cannot be defeated is **(invincible, invincable)**.

b) A corrupt person has been proven **(corruptable, corruptible)**.

c) Evidence that can be admitted in a courtroom is considered **(admissible, admissable)**.

d) If it can be changed, it is **(changeable, changeible)**. 88

Final Silent E before -ING

eyeing or eying?

The root word is **eye**. It ends in **-ye**. You therefore keep the silent final **e** before you add **-ing**. The correct spelling is **(eyeing, eying)**.

147

VI. THE "SEED" WORDS

Do the words with the final sound "seed" end in -ceed, -cede, or -sede?

The only word ending in "seed" is the word "seed."

All other words with that sound end in one of the three ways listed above.

206

---

a) defer

cap

slip

b) regrettable

Review (VII)

a) One who **regrets** is a **(regreter, regretter)**.

b) When you **defy** someone you show **(defyance, defiance)**.

c) When you pretend, are you **shaming** or **shamming**?

d) The bird was **(hiting, hitting)** its beak on the tree.

265

IX. WHEN I PRECEDES E

a) ye

b) ie

c) ai

d) ie

e) i

Do you remember the rule which has been taught in classrooms since great-grandma's day? One phrasing of it is:

Place **i** before **e**
Except after **c**
Or when the sound is **a**
As in **neighbor** or **weigh**.

324

Review of Confusing Sounds

a) sh

b) sounded

c) s

Select the correct answer:

a) The **sh** sound of **c** is found in (**tenacity, tenacious**).

b) What is the root word in **century**?

c) The letter **c** followed by another **c** has the sound (**s, sh, k**).

382

Review (X)

a) slaughter-
house
boughs

b) coughing
roughly

c) toga

a) Which words have the silent **t**?
      custard   nestle   whistle   whist   custom

b) The word with the silent letter is (**unrhymed, trump**).

c) The word with the silent letter is:
      rough   praising   calf   forward

440

Homonyms

a) Who's

whose

shown

b) whose

your and **you're**

Your is a pronoun indicating possession by **you**, either singular or plural. **You're** is the contraction for "you are."

a) (**Your, You're**) certain to drive (**by, bye, buy**) my town house on your way (**to, too**) London.

b) (**Your, You're**) not the person I expected.

498

Review (XII)

a) palatable

b) apparent

c) managing

d) assisting

Correct the **misspelled** word in each group:

a) **busily   happily   prettily   sprily**

b) **truly   unruly   wholy   holy**

c) **potatos   pianos   altos   sopranos**

d) **shoeing   argueing   hoeing   canoeing**

556

Spelling by Sound

yes

You hear them, but they all sound very weak, as the **a** vowel sounds in **dollar**. These are **unaccented vowels**. Words with unaccented vowels are especially hard to spell. They must be studied, for otherwise it is not possible to know just what vowels belong in them.

30

---

a) invincible

b) corruptible

c) admissible

d) changeable

More practice with -able and -ible.

a) A terrible thing can be **(horrable, horrible)**.

b) If you show good sense, you are **(sensable, sensible)**.

c) If you can catch it, it is **(catchible, catchable)**.

d) The person in charge is **(responsable, responsible)**.

e) All this practice has made you **(knowledgeable, knowledgeible)**.

89

---

eyeing

Final Silent E before -ING

a) **Hoeing** or **hoing**?—The root word is **hoe**. It ends in **oe**. The correct spelling is **(hoeing, hoing)**.

b) **Seeing** or **seing**?—The root word is **see**. It ends in **ee**. The correct spelling is **(seeing, seing)**.

c) When you agree, you are **(agreing, agreeing)**.

148

WORDS ENDING IN -CEED

Rule: There are only three words in the English language which end in **-ceed**. They are **proceed, exceed,** and **succeed.**

a) Let us **(proceed, procede, prosede)** to the party.

b) Do not **(exceed, excede, exsede)** the measurements.

c) I hope that you will **(succeed, succede, sucsede)**.

207

---

a) regretter

b) defiance

c) shamming

d) hitting

Review (VII)

Correct the five misspelled words:

I am truely happy to make your acquaintance. I have long prefered active men to those imovable quiet souls who frequent libraries and do little else. It is undenyible that the sucessful record you have made reflects your ability to persevere in action.

266

69

When I Precedes E

Select the correct word:

a) The man who handles cash is a **(casheir, cashier)**.
(Remember: the **ee** sound (as in **see**), calls for **ie**.)

b) Boats dock at a **(pier, peir)**.

c) The leader of the tribe was called the **(chief, cheif)**.

325

Review of Confusing Sounds

Select the correct answer:

a) For a word that follows the pattern of **cemetery**, the correct spelling is **(selery, celery, celary)**.

b) Which is the correct pair for remembering a spelling by association: **(M**ary the secret**ary**, **J**err**ry** the secret**ery)**?

c) A rising elevator is **(asending, ascending)**. 383

a) tenacious

b) cent

c) k

Review (X)

a) The word with a silent letter is **(almond, full-masted)**.

b) The word with the silent **gh** is **(thorough, rough)**.

c) The silent **b** is in the word **(symbol, lambs)**.

d) The **t** is silent in **(bristle, lasting, twisted)**.

441

a) nestle
whistle

b) unrhymed

c) calf

---

rain, reign, and rein

Rain refers to the water falling from clouds, and the act of falling freely, as rain water does.

Reign (the noun) refers to the time during which a sovereign rules.

Reins refers to leather straps used by a rider or driver to control the head of an animal. **Reins** can also refer to command, such as "the reins of power." 499

a) You're
by
to

b) You're

Review (XII)

Which word in each group is **correctly** spelled?

a) **alright   patiently   surounded   packking**

b) **atheletic   embarassed   hinges   knowlidge**

c) **afected   succesful   aweful   deference**

d) **chasm   charakter   docter   preparring**

557

a) spryly

b) wholly

c) potatoes

d) arguing

70

REMEMBER: To spell a word correctly, you must:
LISTEN to the word.
LOOK at the word.
SAY the word and
NOTE any unusual feature of the word.

31

Adjective Suffixes

a) horrible
b) sensible
c) catchable
d) responsible
e) knowledge-
   able

Use **-able** if the root ends in hard **c** or hard **g.**
Navigable, not navigible
Amicable, not amicible
a) A hateful thing is **(despicable, despicible).**
   (The **c** has the hard sound, as in **cat.**)
b) If it is perfect in appearance, it is **(impeccible, impeccable).**

90

Select the correct spelling:
a) The blacksmith knows all about **(shoing, shoeing).**

a) hoeing

b) seeing

c) agreeing

b) His shoes wore out because he was **(toing, toeing)** in.
c) Tyrants are known for their **(decreing, decreeing)** of harsh laws and regulations.
d) The **(fleeing, fleing)** thieves were not **(loveable, lovable).**

149

WORDS ENDING IN -SEDE

a) proceed

b) exceed

c) succeed

Rule: The only word in the English language that ends with **-sede** is **supersede.** It means "to take the place of" or "to take precedence over."
If you **(excede, exsede, exceed)** your authority, it will be necessary for the government to appoint someone to **(supercede, supersede, superceed)** you.

208

truly

preferred

immovable

undeniable

successful

Review (VII)

a) Can you determine the root word of **impassable?**
b) Is one who has been killed **slayn** or **slain?**
c) If something is **excessive,** does it **excede** or **exceed** its proper limits?
d) Speaking of **limits,** is a boundless distance **ilimitable** or **illimitable?**

267

71

a) cashier

b) pier

c) chief

When I Precedes E

Select the correct word:

a) The ideas you hold are called your (beleifs, beliefs).

b) beleivable beleiveable believable believeable?

c) recieving reciving receiveing receiving?

326

---

a) celery

b) Mary the secretary

c) ascending

Review of Confusing Sounds

a) The **g** is silent in each of these words except:
   signer designing reigning signature

b) The word with a silent letter is:
   chaos handwritten vicious parted

384

---

a) almond

b) thorough

c) lambs

d) bristle

A SPECIAL REVIEW: DOUBLE CONSONANTS

The following questions will test your ability to determine when a final consonant is to be doubled before the addition of a suffix. If you make 3 or more errors, go back to Chapter VII and study it again.

One who bats the ball is the (bater, batter).

442

Homonyms

Select the correct word:

a) Elizabeth (reins, reigns) over a happy people who support her (holy, wholly).

b) Presents (reigned, rained) upon the princess when she celebrated her birthday.

c) The general assumed the (reigns, reins) of government.

500

---

a) patiently

b) hinges

c) deference

d) chasm

Review (XII)

Which word in each group contains one or more silent letters?

a) **importantly speedily vaguely regularly**

b) **interregnum condign dignity signify**

c) **subtlety preparation teeming handily**

d) **condemnatory damnably solemnity limning**

558

SYLLABLES

be-gin   help-ing   a-way   re-peat   pre-vent
Each of these words is made up of two different sounds. The hyphen divides each word into its two sounds. The group of letters which represents a sound is called a **syllable**. These words are called two-syllable words. How many syllables are there in the word **interfere?**   32

Adjective Suffixes

Use **-ible** if the root ends in soft **c** or soft **g**.
                    Force becomes **forcible**

a) despicable

b) impeccable

a) Since the **g** is soft, the correct spelling is **(legable, legible)**.
b) Anything you can reduce is **(reducible, reducable)**.   91

a) shoeing

b) toeing

c) decreeing

d) fleeing

   lovable

Select the correct spelling:
a) Every gardener should be adept at **(hoing, hoeing)**.
b) Why is he **(guaranteeing, guaranteing)** this old clock?
c) No **(arguement, argument)** is possible, for I know that he is still **(lying, lieing)** in his bed.
d) His greatest joy lies in **(treeing, treing)** the fox. 150

WORDS ENDING IN -CEDE
conseed, consede, conceed, or **concede?**

exceed

supersede

Rule: Except for the four words **proceed, exceed, succeed,** and **supersede,** and the words including the idea "seed," all other words ending in the "seed" sound are spelled with **-cede**.
If you insist, I will **(conceed, consede, concede)** the victory and resign the game.   209

a) pass

b) slain

c) exceed

d) illimitable

a) Any hillside can be considered **(erodeable, erodable)**.
b) The sowing of seed is soon followed by **(hoing, hoeing)**.
c) Correct the mistake in: "We will **procede** to secede."
d) The root word is **compliant**. Is the related noun **compliance** or **complience?**   268

73

When I Precedes E

a) beliefs

b) believable

c) receiving

Select the correct word:
a) **decciving   deceiveing   decieving   decieveing**
b) **concieveable   concievable   conceivable   conceiveable**
c) **reprciving   repreiveing   reprieveing   reprieving**

327

REVIEW (X)

a) signature

b) handwritten

a) The root word is **service**. Do you retain the final **e** when adding **-ing**, or when adding **-able**?
b) The word **trued** is used by mechanics. In making this word, the final **e** of **true** has been **(dropped, retained)**.
c) "The golfer **teed** off." The final **e** of the root was **(dropped, retained)**.

385

batter

Select the correct spelling:
a) When something does not continue, it is **(stoped, stopped)**.
b) To be given permission is to be **(permited, permitted)**.
c) If you do not want something seen, you must keep it **(hiden, hidden)**.
d) Those who made a profit had **(profited, profitted)**.

443

Homonyms

a) reigns

   wholly

b) rained

c) reins

way and **weigh**

Way refers to a method of doing something, or to a route—as "the way home."
Weigh refers to the determination of heaviness or of importance.
Weightiness means **importance**.

501

a) vaguely

b) condign

c) subtlety

d) limning

Review (XII)

a) Which is correct **(paid** or **payed)**?
b) What is the plural of **scarf**?
c) Is it **complection** or **complexion**?
d) What is the plural of the fish named **cod**?

559

3
in-ter-fere

A Spelling Rule:
Every syllable contains at least one vowel.
"O-pen wide," re-peat-ed the hap-py den-tist."
Notice that every syllable in this sentence contains at least one vowel. Here is a three-syllable word. Divide the word into its syllables, and then find the vowel or vowels in each syllable.

chemistry **33**

---

a) legible

b) reducible

Adjective Suffixes
a) The soft **c** makes the correct spelling **(irascable, irascible).**
b) But the hard **c** makes the word meaning that something can be explained **(explicable, explicible).**
c) The soft **c** in its sound makes the word meaning "easily mixed" **(miscable, miscible).** **92**

---

a) hoeing

b) guaranteeing

c) argument

lying

d) treeing

REVIEW (IV)
Remember—you cannot improve your spelling by reading through this book once, and then forgetting about it.
Something of which you do not approve receives your **(disapproveal, disapproval).** **151**

---

concede

The "Seed" Words
Select the correct word:
a) You may ask me not to interfere in this matter, but I feel I must **(interceed, intercede, intersede).**
b) I promise never to **(excede, exceed)** the speed limits.
c) Several minor officials **(presede, precede, preceed)** the minister into the chamber. **210**

---

a) erodable

b) hoeing

c) proceed

d) compliance

Review (VII)
a) The fighter was knocked **(insensible, insensable).**
b) I find your help **(indispensible, indispensable).**
c) The villain's actions are **(reprehensible, reprehensable).**
d) How many of the decisions are **(defensible, defensable)?** **269**

When I Precedes E

a) deceiving

b) conceivable

c) reprieving

Select the correct word:

a) The end of the heat wave was a great (releif, relief).

b) The miner had found a rich (vien, vein) of ore.

c) The railroad cars were loaded with (freight, frieght).

328

---

a) -ing (no)

  -able (yes)

b) dropped

c) dropped

a) The director expects you to be most (dutyful, dutiful).

b) I've had enough of your (silliness, sillyness).

c) Would you prefer to observe my (coiness, coyness)?

d) Our food supplies are (plentiful, plentyful).

e) How many eggs has the hen already (layed, laid)?

386

Review—Double Consonants

a) stopped

b) permitted

c) hidden

d) profited

Select the correct spelling:

a) When you fail to remember, you have (forgoten, forgotten).

b) The start is called the (begining, beginning).

c) Something detestable is (abhored, abhorred).

d) To be forced is to be (compeled, compelled).

444

Homonyms

a) Please (way, weigh) the possible results before you decide on the (way, weigh) you will act.

b) Balance the scales this (way, weigh) to make them (weigh, way) accurately.

c) His honest actions show that he believes in an upright (way, weigh) of life.

502

---

a) paid

b) scarves

c) complexion

d) cod

Review (XII)

a) What is the singular of **elves?**

b) I want to know what (occured, occurred).

c) The lawyer smiled and (demured, demurred).

d) The doctor pronounced the child (cured, curred).

560

chem-is-try

Syllables

Divide each of these words into its syllables. Then indicate the vowel or vowels in each syllable.

simplify   underline   duplicate

34

REVIEW (II)

a) irascible

b) explicable

c) miscible

Three of the designated words are misspelled. Identify them and write them correctly.

The **innocent** man showed great **intelligance** in proving that the young **adolescent** had been guilty of deliberate **negligance** in upsetting the **magnificant** house of cards.

93

---

disapproval

Review (IV)

a) When a word ends in a final silent **e**, the **e** is usually (retained, dropped) before adding a suffix beginning with a vowel.

b) A place in which workers **refine** oil is called a (**refineing, refining**) center.

152

---

a) intercede

b) exceed

c) precede

Select the correct word:

a) I doubt that he can ever (**succeed, sucsede**).

b) Why do you (**procede, proceed**) so cautiously?

c) This regulation will of necessity (**supercede, supersede**) all previous rules and practices.

d) There is some talk that the local branch plans to (**scccced, sccede**) from the national organization.

211

---

a) insensible

b) indispensable

c) reprehensible

d) defensible

Review (VII)

a) Be careful of your (**spacing, spaceing**).

b) Which of these words have verb roots?

international indefinable regrettable dependable

c) A lion that **roars** is obviously a (**roaring, roarring**) beast.

d) Your work is at last (**improving, improveing**).

270

77

a) relief

b) vein

c) freight

When I Precedes E

Select the correct word:

a) I think they are **(thiefs, theifs, thieves, theives)**.

b) This is a wonderful **(acheivement, achievement)**!

c) The highest part of the room is the **(cieling, ceiling)**.

329

---

a) dutiful

b) silliness

c) coyness

d) plentiful

e) laid

a) Officer, this man has been **(slayn, slain)**!

b) People always complain about desert **(driness, dryness)**.

c) When his leg healed, he walked about **(spryly, sprily)**.

d) This is a perfect day for **(flying, fliing)**.

e) It is a fact which is **(undenyable, undeniable)**.

387

---

a) forgotten

b) beginning

c) abhorred

d) compelled

Review—Double Consonants

Select the correct spelling:

a) Every package should be **(unwraped, unwrapped)**.

b) Something left out is **(omited, omitted)**.

c) The prices of some items are **(controled, controlled)** by law.

d) Making reference to something is the art of **(refering, referring)** to it.

445

---

a) weigh

way

b) way

weigh

c) way

forth and **fourth**

Forth is a little-used word meaning "forward," "out of," or "as a result of." It appears in the phrase "and so forth," meaning "and on and on," or "et cetera." **Fourth** refers to the numerical position after **third**.

The **(forth, fourth)** knight then came **(forth, fourth)**.

503

---

a) elf

b) occurred

c) demurred

d) cured

Review (XII)

a) The cat closed its eyes and **(pured, purred)**.

b) I fell into the trap into which I had been **(lured, lurred)**.

c) Of all the members, he is the **(lazyest, laziest)**.

d) Of all the animals, the fox is the **(sliest, slyest)**.

561

sim-pli-fy

un-der-line

du-pli-cate

improve   unable   disappear   return
The syllables **im-**, **un-**, **dis-**, and **re-** in these words are called **prefixes**. A **prefix** is a syllable placed at the beginning of a word. It usually gives a special meaning to that word. Can you find the two words in the group below which have prefixes?

unable   hollow   running   unwind   robber   35

Review (II)

intelligence

negligence

magnificent

Three of the designated words are misspelled. Identify them and write them correctly.

Underground **resistence** during the war showed how **persistent** was the popular **insistence** on freedom. After all, people whose **subsistance** had been threatened by an **adjacant** nation could not just give up.   94

Review (IV)

a) dropped

b) refining

a) The artist feels that the dirt smear on the painting is **(removable, removeable)**.
b) The cigar lay on the ground, still **(smokeing, smoking)**.
c) The unruly students knew that their master would lose little time in **(reproveing, reproving)** them.   153

---

a) succeed

b) proceed

c) supersede

d) secede

Select the correct word:
a) Two days later, the flood waters began to **(receed, recede)**.
b) If one event occurs before another, we say that the first **(anteceeds, antecedes)** the second.
c) The strike had been on for ten days before the management decided to **(accede, acceed)** to their plea.   212

---

a) spacing
b) indefinable
   regrettable
   dependable

c) roaring

d) improving

Review (VII)

Select and correct the misspelled word in each group.
a) **cropping   slipping   ropping   dipping**
b) **fatter   batter   sitter   eatter**
c) **succede   precede   secede   recede**
d) **peaceable   forceible   lacing   racing**   271

When I Precedes E

a) thieves

b) achievement

c) ceiling

Select the correct word:

a) In religion the opposite of a **layman** is a **(preist, priest)**.

b) He was born during Victoria's **(riegn, reign)**.

c) The flour is passed through a **(seive, sieve)**.

d) The gallant knight raised his **(shield, sheild)**.

330

---

a) slain

b) dryness

c) spryly

d) flying

e) undeniable

Review (X)

a) The population of South America may in time **(excede, exceed, exseed)** that of Europe.

b) Will you **(intercede, intersede)** in my behalf?

c) Is it **proceedure** or **procedure**?

d) How many words end in **-sede**?

388

---

a) unwrapped

b) omitted

c) controlled

d) referring

Select the correct spelling:

a) Something not allowed is **(forbiden, forbidden)**.

b) A group organized for a special purpose is a **(comitee, commitee, committee)**.

c) To be allowed to enter is to be granted **(admitance, admittance)**.

d) One who does something over again is a **(repeater, repeatter)**.

446

Homonyms

patients and patience

fourth

forth

Patients are the persons treated by a physician or dentist. **Patience** is the willingness or ability to wait.

a) He shows great **(patients, patience)** in treating his nervous **(patients, patience)**.

b) Have you ever seen so much **(patients, patience)?**

504

---

a) purred

b) lured

c) laziest

d) slyest

Review (XII)

a) Of all the clowns, he is the **(siliest, silliest, sillyest)**.

b) Of all the recent days, this is the **(chilliest, chillyest)**.

c) Of all the evil men, he is the **(vileest, vilest)**.

d) Is it **impudance** or **impudence**?

562

Prefixes

unable

unwind

A prefix is always a syllable. It always comes at the beginning of a word. You can always recognize that a first syllable is a prefix if you are left with a complete word when you take away the first syllable. What is the prefix in each of these words?

unpopular   report   detail

36

Review (II)

resistance

subsistence

adjacent

a) Find the verb which is the root of each of the words listed below:

interference   preference   transference

b) Which three of these words have verb roots? The **refusal** of the **hiker** was **caused** by his **stupidity**.

95

Review (IV)

a) removable

b) smoking

c) reproving

a) The handkerchief had a scent which was just **(defineable, definable)**.

b) Which is correct, **telephoner** or **telephoneer**?

c) He feels that his **(loseing, losing)** of the game was caused by your **(chasing, chaseing)** his ball.

d) The musician was busy **(composing, composeing)** a new song.

154

---

succeeded or **succeded?**

a) recede

b) antecedes

c) accede

Rule: "Seed" words follow their normal spelling when suffixes are added. A final **e** follows the usual rules.

The normal correct spelling is **succeed.** The addition of the suffix **-ed** does not change this spelling. The correct spelling is therefore **(succeeded, succeded).**

213

---

a) roping

b) eater

c) succeed

d) forcible

Review (VII)

Which word in each line is **correctly** spelled?

a) **hazing   blazeing   crazyest   hazyest**

b) **purness   vagueness   happyness   finness**

c) **easly   funnyly   wryly   slily**

d) **resistent   insistent   significant   defience**

272

a) priest

b) reign

c) sieve

d) shield

When I Precedes E

either or iether?

Exceptions to the -ie rule: Reading and writing would be so much simpler if the English language would only follow its own rules. But it doesn't. Here are five exceptions which you must memorize:

either neither seize weird leisure

331

---

a) exceed

b) intercede

c) procedure

d) one—

supersede

Review (X)

a) Which is correct, **leaped** or **leapped?**

b) The mattress is filled with cotton **(bating, batting).**

c) One popular winter sport is **(tobogganing, tobogganning).**

d) Why are you **(staring, starring)** at me, madam?

389

---

a) forbidden

b) committee

c) admittance

d) repeater

Select the correct spelling:

a) The act of showing something is **(revealing, revealling)** it.

b) One not satisfied is usually **(complaining, complainning).**

c) Have you heard the story of the wicked king who was **(beheaded, beheadded)?**

d) When will this shoe be **(repaired, repairred)?**   447

---

a) patience

patients

b) patience

Homonyms

died and dyed   dying and dyeing

Died is the past form of the verb "to die." **Dyed** is the past form of "to dye," meaning "to color or stain." The -ing forms are **dying** and **dyeing.**

505

---

a) silliest

b) chilliest

c) vilest

d) impudence

Review (XII)

a) Is it **innocance** or **innocence?**

b) Which is correct, **resistance** or **resistence?**

c) Which is correct, **appearance** or **appearence?**

d) Does one act **persistantly** or **persistently?**

563

Prefixes

repeat   **im**pose   **dis**gust   **en**trap

unpopular

report

detail

Sometimes a prefix is placed before a word to give it a special meaning. In other cases, it is placed before the **root** of a word (the basic form of a word). You do not have to know many roots to spell well, but you should learn to recognize the common prefixes.   **37**

---

a) interfere
  prefer
  transfer
b) refusal
  hiker
  caused

Review (II)

All of the words in each group should end in either **-able** or **-ible.** Which should it be for each group?
a) **admir**......, **imagin**......, **navig**......, **dur**.......
b) **pass**......, **demonstr**......, **siz**......, **laugh**......
c) **poss**......, **vis**......, **invinc**......, **admiss**......

96

---

a) definable
b) telephoner
c) losing
  chasing
d) composing

Review (IV)

Add the indicated suffix to the root word.
a) **-ness: Fine** becomes..................
b) **-less: Use** becomes..................
c) **-ful: Grate** (from gratitude) becomes..............
d) **-like: Mouse** becomes.................

155

---

succeeded

Select the correct word:
a) I was amazed to read that the **(procedings, proceedings)** in the trials had required four months.
b) The **(receeding, receding)** mob left many dead behind.
c) I was angry at the club president for **(superseding, superceding)** me in this important matter. **214**

---

a) hazing
b) vagueness
c) wryly
d) insistent

Review (VII)

a) Is a hurricane described as **rageing** or **raging**?
b) Do you make **payments** or **paiments** on a debt?
c) If an action is not **legal**, is it **ilegal** or **illegal**?
d) Is a harmful action a **diservice** or a **disservice**?

273

either   seize   weird   leisure

Place these words in the proper spaces in the paragraph below.

The choice was mine. I could select .... one of the .... costumes. If I won with it at the ball, I could look forward to a life of .... I reached for one, but slipped and fell just as I was about to .... it.

332

---

a) leaped

b) batting

c) tobogganing

d) staring

Review (X)

a) The villain was sentenced to be **(floged, flogged)**.

b) From **confer** we get **conferred** and **(conference, conferrence)**.

c) How long have your headaches been **(occurring, occuring)**.

d) Are you **referring** to my **(referrance, reference)?**

390

---

a) revealing

b) complaining

c) beheaded

d) repaired

Review—Double Consonants

Select the correct spelling:

a) He stood there without **(uttering, utterring)** a word.

b) I watched him strut as he was **(entering, enterring)**.

c) Lifeguards must be good **(swimers, swimmers)**.

448

Homonyms

died and **dyed**   **dying** and **dyeing**

a) The blood of the **(dying, dyeing)** man was flowing.

b) The artist **(died, dyed)** before the cloth was **(died, dyed)**.

c) The beauty of the colors of this painting is **(undying, undyeing)**.

506

---

a) innocence

b) resistance

c) appearance

d) persistently

Review (XII)

Select the correct word.

a) I find him to be most **(unruely, unruly)**.

b) How many men did you say were **(slayed, slayn, slain)?**

c) His manner was surprisingly **(amicible, amicable)**.

d) He is considered to be **(horrible, horrable)**.

564

SUFFIXES

walk**ing** jump**er** halt**ed** part**ies**
The syllables **-ing, -er, -ed,** and **-ies** in these words
are called **suffixes.** A **suffix** is a syllable placed at
the end of a word (or at the end of a root). It
usually gives a special meaning to that word.

38

---

a) -able

b) -able

c) -ible

Review (II)

Correct the one misspelled word in each group.
- *a)* **collectible   passible   impossible   sensible**
- *b)* **imaginable   portable   credable   admirable**
- *c)* **eatable   convertable   laughable   deplorable**
- *d)* **audible   visible   impeccable   despicible**
- *e)* **legible   horrable   eligible   desirable**

97

---

a) fineness

b) useless

c) grateful

d) mouselike

Review (IV)

a) The fact that the word **service** ends in a soft **c**
followed by a silent **e** makes the correct spelling
(serviceable, servicable).

b) Some retired generals have made poor public
officials because they do not always seek
(peacable, peaceable) solutions to world problems.

156

---

a) proceedings

b) receding

c) superseding

The "Seed" Words

Correct the three words which are incorrect.
It was a delicate matter. I could scarcely **conceed**
his right to the property without **proceding** to leave
it. Nevertheless, I knew he would have little
difficulty in getting the police to **intercede** in his
behalf. I took the only possible course, and
acceeded to his offer.

215

---

a) raging

b) payments

c) illegal

d) disservice

Review (VII)

a) The chairman of the **(commitee, committee)** was
(busyly, busily) **(phoneing, phoning)** most of the
day.

b) He was more **(couragous, courageous)** than any
other man I have ever known.

c) I have never heard of such **(intolerence, intolerance)**!

274

85

When I Precedes E

a) either	**either neither seize weird leisure**
	Select the correct word from those above:
b) weird	*a)* The word used to describe **grasping** is...............
c) leisure	*b)* The word which implies a positive **choice** is...............
d) seize	*c)* The word meaning **unusual** or **strange** is..........
	d) The word with a **negative** meaning is............. **333**

Review (X)

a) flogged	*a)* The plural of **echo** is **(echos, echoes).**
b) conference	*b)* The plural of **sentry** is **(sentries, sentrys).**
c) occurring	*c)* The dog appreciates these **(careses, caresses).**
d) reference	*d)* Which of these words is incorrect? Correct it.
	halves knives loaves gulves
	391

Review—Double Consonants

a) uttering	Select the correct spelling:
b) entering	*a)* This metal closing is called a **(ziper, zipper).**
	b) Something desired is something **(wanted, wantted).**
c) swimmers	*c)* A violin out of tune needs **(tuning, tunning).**
	449

	Select the correct word:
a) dying	*a)* The teacher is a man of high **(principals, principles).**
b) died	*b)* He set **(forth, fourth)** into the wilderness.
dyed	*c)* **(Your, You're)** the one **(who's, whose)** **(way, weigh)** of measuring results is being questioned.
c) undying	*d)* Now the railing will be **(stationary, stationery).**
	507

Review (XII)

a) unruly	Select the correct word.
b) slain	*a)* I saw the sick man **(reclining, reclineing)** nearby.
c) amicable	*b)* This house has a **(sizable, sizeable)** **(morgage, mortgage).**
d) horrible	*c)* I have been grossly **(decieved, deceived).**
	565

Suffixes

Can you find the two words in the group below which have suffixes?

> decided   return   eating   walks

39

---

a) passable

b) credible

c) convertible

d) despicable

e) horrible

III. AVOIDING TROUBLES WITH PREFIXES

A General Rule: Prefixes do not change the spelling of the words to which they are added.

disappear or dissappear?

The prefix is **dis-,** meaning **not.** It is added to the word **appear.** Prefixes do not change the spelling of the words to which they are added. The correct spelling is therefore **(disappear, dissappear).**   **98**

Review (IV)

a) serviceable

b) peaceable

a) The fact that the word **change** ends in a soft **g** followed by a silent **e** makes the correct spelling **(changable, changeable).**

b) The queen is **(arranging, arrangeing)** for the finest of all **(arrangable, arrangeable)** parties.

c) The missing gems were **(untraceable, untracable).** **157**

The "Seed" Words

concede

proceeding

acceded

Which sentence is **without** errors?

a) Exceding the limits will not help you succeed.

b) The builder proceeded, despite the known problems.

c) It is incredable that you should dare to super-cede his authority in this matter! **216**

---

a) committee

busily

phoning

b) courageous

c) intolerance

Review (VII)

a) If you compel someone to do something, has he been **compeled** or **compelled**?

b) Correct the form of the word **shag** which is incorrectly spelled.

> **shagging**   **shaged**   **shaggily**   **shagginess**

c) A canoe with a special timber to prevent tipping is called an **(outriger, outrigger).** **275**

When I Precedes E

a) seize

b) either

c) weird

d) neither

Select the correct word:
a) The army garrison was finally (releived, relieved).
b) (Niether, neither) of the recipes was successful.
c) The hungry wolf followed the (sleigh, sliegh).
d) He is a gentleman of (liesure, leisure).
e) The frightened woman awoke with a (shriek, shreik).

334

Review (X)

a) echoes

b) sentries

c) caresses

d) gulfs

Correct the **incorrect** plural in each group:
a) **beaver gooses charts laces**
b) **childs mice sheriffs throngs**
c) **potatos radios altos pianos**
d) **deer sheep halibuts cats**

392

Review—Double Consonants

a) zipper

b) wanted

c) tuning

Select the correct spelling:
a) The rabbit was examined before (skining, skinning).
b) The doctor was pleased when the child was (cured, curred).
c) He received the support of his (backers, backkers).

450

Homonyms

a) principles

b) forth

c) You're
whose
way

d) stationary

pear, pair, and **pare**

Pear is the fruit; **pair** means "two of a kind"; **pare** means "to peel, usually by cutting off an outer layer."
a) Please send me a (pear, pair, pare) of (pears, pairs, pares).
b) (Pear, Pair, Pare) the fruit before cooking it.

508

Review (XII)

a) reclining

b) sizable
mortgage

c) deceived

Select the correct word.
a) I do not desire (either, iether) book you offer.
b) This flat land is a typical (plain, plane).
c) The gold was located in a rich (vane, vein, vain).
d) The football team has good (morale, moral).

566

Prefixes and Suffixes

decided

eating

returning   happily   unsure   **grown**
a) Some words have suffixes (happily).
b) Some words have prefixes (unsure).
c) Some words have both suffixes **and** prefixes (returning).
d) Some words have **no** suffixes and **no** prefixes (grown).   40

---

disappear

un- mis- anti- con- de- in- inter- re-
These are some of the more common prefixes. When you add them, the spelling of the original word is not changed.
a) **Dis-** (meaning not) added to **satisfied** becomes
....
b) **Im-** (meaning not) added to **mortal** becomes
....   99

---

a) changeable

b) arranging

   arrangeable

c) untraceable

Review (IV)

a) My lord, you speak **(truely, truly).**
b) The cracked platters are not **(usable, useable).**
c) I remember him but **(vaguely, vaguly).**
d) Why are you two old friends **(argueing, arguing)?**
e) I am in **awe** of his **(aweful, awful)** anger.   158

---

b)

The "Seed" Words

Which sentence contains an error in spelling?
a) The dying man had succeeded in completing his will.
b) Your defyance forces me to intercede.
c) The ruins remaining when the waters receded left us at a loss as to how to proceed.   217

---

a) compelled

b) shagged

c) outrigger

Review (VII)

a) The corpse was **(duly, duely) (interred, intered).**
b) The nurse wasted no time in **(transmiting, transmitting)** the information to the doctors.
c) I have never known a woman who would deliberately act so **(unpleasently, unpleasantly).**   276

a) relieved
b) Neither
c) sleigh
d) leisure
e) shriek

When I Precedes E
Let's change the rhyme into three simple rules:
Rule: Write **ie** when the sound is **ee** (as in **see**), except after **c**.
Rule: Write **ei** when the sound is **ee**, if it follows **c**.
Rule: Write **ei** when the sound is **a**.
Yeild or **yield**? The sound is **ee**. The correct spelling is **(yeild, yield)**. 335

---

a) geese
b) children
c) potatoes
d) halibut

a) Shorter working hours can mean more **(liesure, leisure)**.
b) He would speak only **(briefly, breifly)**.
c) Nobody enjoys being **(decieved, deceived)**.
d) Yellow Hand was an Apache **(cheiftain, chieftain)**.
e) This is certainly a **(wierd, weird)** tale! 393

XI. HOMONYMS

a) skinning
b) cured
c) backers

Homonyms are words that have the same sound, but different meanings and different spellings. Confusion in spelling results when you are not certain of the meaning of the words in a pair or trio of homonyms. This chapter will deal with the homonyms most useful in everyday life. 451

---

a) pair
   pears
b) Pare

accept and **except** (not homonyms if pronounced correctly)
Remember that the first sounds differ; the **a** in **accept** is like the **a** in **hat**, while the **e** in **except** is like the **e** in **pet**. **Accept** means "to take or to agree with"; **except** is used to indicate that something has been left out. 509

---

a) either
b) plain
c) vein
d) morale

Review (XII)
Correct the 5 **misspelled** or **incorrectly used** words: I find my friends to easily fooled by knaves who seem respectable but are really theives. They beleive whatever they hear, and think that there luck is perfect. I canot understand what is wrong with them! 567

Prefixes and Suffixes

a) Which two of these words have prefixes?
unsure   walking   conduct

b) Which two of these words have suffixes?
training   twisted   letters

41

Prefixes

Adding a prefix does not change the spelling of the original word.

a) dissatisfied

b) immortal

a) **Dis-** plus **approve** becomes..................

b) **Il-** (meaning not) added to **literate** (being able to read and write) becomes..................

c) **Im-** (meaning not) plus **movable** becomes ....

100

---

a) truly

b) usable

c) vaguely

d) arguing

e) awful

Review (IV)

a) Since the word **lie** ends in the letters **-ie**, the correct form becomes **(lieing, lying).**

b) The battlefield was filled with **(dieing, dying)** men.

c) They say that the surprise witness **(lied, lyed).**

d) He felt **(tongue-tyed, tongue-tied)** before the court.

159

---

b)

The "Seed" Words

proceedure or **procedure?**

Rule: Never use a double **e** when writing a related word based on one of the "seed" words.

Proceed is one of the words which contains a double **e.** We do not use the double **e** when spelling related words. The correct spelling is therefore **(proceedure, procedure).**

218

---

a) duly

interred

b) transmitting

c) unpleasantly

Review (VII)

a) Why should we **confer** about it? There is nothing to be gained by another **(conference, conference).**

b) Yes, I'll **defer** to the judge, for he merits such **(deference, deferrence).**

c) The threat of prison is a strong **(deterent, deterrent).**

277

When I Precedes E

niece or neice?   breif or brief?

a) Since the sound is **ee**, the correct spelling is with **ie**, and the answer is **(niece, neice)**.

b) Since the sound is **ee**, the correct spelling is with **ie**, and the answer is **(breif, brief)**.

336

a) leisure

b) briefly

c) deceived

d) chieftain

e) weird

Review (X)

a) Which of these pairs is **correct: neither, siezure; neither, siezure; niether, seizure; neither, seizure?**

b) Which of these is **correct: the relieved soveriegn; the inconceivable deciet; the conceited heavyweight; the mischeivous foreigner?**

394

Homonyms

blue and blew

The correct uses are indicated in these sentences:

a) I have a **blue** dress.

b) The wind **blew** my hat away.

Use **blue** when you mean the color. Use **blew** when you mean the result of wind pressure.

Do you use **blueing** or **blewing** in the wash? 452

accept and except

a) I will **(accept, except)** the money.

b) I cannot make an **(acception, exception)**, even though I can well **(accept, except)** your reason for requesting one.

510

too

thieves

believe

their

cannot

Review (XII)

Select the correct word:

a) Your position is **(indefensible, indefensable)**.

b) The brave soldier was **(dubed, dubbed)** a knight.

c) I am going to fish for **(tuna, tunas)**.

568

92

Syllables

a) **un**sure

conduct

b) train**ing**

twist**ed**

A good speller learns to divide words into syllables.
Learn these rules for dividing words:
a) A prefix is a separate syllable.
b) A suffix is a separate syllable, sometimes two.
c) When you have two consonants between two vowels, you usually make the division between the consonants.

42

---

a) disapprove

b) illiterate

c) immovable

a) **Un-** (meaning not) added to **natural** becomes
....

Remember: Adding a prefix does not change the spelling.

b) **Anti** ... added to the root **dote** becomes ....

c) **In-** means not. If something is not correct, it is
.... (Just add the prefix.)

d) **Mis-** (meaning in error) plus **sent** becomes......... 101

Review (IV)

a) lying

b) dying

c) lied

d) tongue-tied

a) The man with the **hoe** was busy **(hoing, hoeing).**

b) The blacksmith was intent on **(reshoeing, reshoing)** the rebellious horse.

c) The captain was happy after **(freing, freeing)** his captives.

d) He was standing near the case **(eying, eyeing)** the jewels.

160

---

procedure

Select the correct word:
a) We **(proceded, proceeded)** to select the correct **(proceess, process).**

b) Those who succeed deserve their **(success, succeess).**

c) The boys recited in **(succeession, succession).**

d) You ask me to concede! Sir, I will never make the slightest **(conceesion, concession).**

219

VIII. PLURALS OF NOUNS

a) conference

b) deference

c) deterrent

house—houses? **machine—machines?**
Rule: Most nouns form their plurals by adding the letter **s** to the singular form of the noun. Such nouns can be referred to as "regular" nouns.
The plural of **book** is therefore **(bookes, books).**

278

93

When I Precedes E

nieghbor or **neighbor?** **piece** or **peice?**

a) niece

a) Since the sound is **not ee**, the correct spelling is with **ei**, and the answer is **(nieghbor, neighbor)**.

b) brief

b) Since the sound is **ee**, the correct spelling is with **ie**, and the answer is **(piece, peice)**.

337

Review (X)

a) neither, seizure

a) Correct the misspelled word:
leisurely height veiwpoint deficient

b) the conceited heavyweight

b) Always treat children with **(pateince, patience)**.

c) The edict was directed against all **(priests, preists)**.

395

---

break and **brake**

a) I will **break** the stick into two parts.

b) The automobile has good **brakes**.

blueing

Remember that the word **brake** means a stopping of some sort.

c) He is not the one to **(break, brake)** his word.

d) This lever will help you **(break, brake)** the sled.

453

---

affect and **effect** (not homonyms if pronounced correctly)

a) accept

Use **affect** when you want to show one thing influencing another; use **effect** when you want to show the result of such influencing.

b) exception

accept

a) What is the **(affect, effect)** of this medicine?

b) How does this medicine **(affect, effect)** the patient?

511

Review (XII)

a) indefensible

Which word in each line has the indicated silent letter(s)?

b) dubbed

a) **gh** ghostly tougher laughter slighter

c) tuna

b) **n** signer solemnly feigning gnash

c) **b** thumbs crumble ambling symbol

d) **t** astern pestilence restful nestled

569

94

pub-lish (two consonants between two vowels)
ex-port (two consonants between two vowels)
Divide the words below into syllables, following the rule for words in which there are "two consonants between two vowels."

burden   splendid   invent

43

---

a) unnatural

b) antidote

c) incorrect

d) missent

Prefixes
a) Something which has been spelled incorrectly has been **(mispelled, misspelled)**.
b) Combining **re-** (meaning again or over again) and **write** gives the word ....
c) Using the word **over** as a prefix for the word **run** gives you the word ....

102

---

a) hoeing

b) reshoeing

c) freeing

d) eyeing

Review (IV)
Did you make many mistakes in this series of review frames? Each mistake means that you should restudy the frames tested by the review questions. Do not go on to Frame 162 until you have assured yourself of the mastery of all the frames that came before.

161

---

a) proceeded

process

b) success

c) succession

d) concession

The "Seed" Words
Select the correct word:
a) This and the **(succeessive, successive)** chapters complete the tale of the successful treasure hunt.
b) Something which comes before something else is called its **(antecedent, anteceedent)**.
c) A business decline is called a **(receession, recession)**.

220

REGULAR NOUN PLURALS

books

a) Write the plural of each of these words:
stick   dance   fan   basket
b) To form the plural of a regular noun add the letter ...... to its singular form.
c) Nouns which are not regular will be given the name **(iregular, irregular)**.

279

When I Precedes E

a) neighbor

b) piece

Select the correct word:

a) Is the person to whom an inheritance is left the **hier** or the **heir**? (Is the sound **ee**)?

b) **Recieve** or **receive**? The sound is **ee**, but it follows the letter **c**. This makes the correct spelling **(recieve, receive)**.

338

THE SILENT B

a) viewpoint

b) patience

c) priests

dum or dumb?

Rule: The letter **b** is usually silent after **m** in the **same syllable.** The **b** still remains silent if a suffix is added, since suffixes are separate syllables.

a) Do you hear the letter **b** in **dumb?**

b) Do you hear the letter **b** in **climbing?**

396

Homonyms

c) break

d) brake

All ways and always

Always has the meaning "at all times." The phrase **all ways** is used to indicate that something can be performed by a variety of methods. Never use **all ways** when you are referring to time.

454

Homonyms

a) effect

b) affect

Select the correct word:

a) His army career had the **(effect, affect)** of changing his personality.

b) How was the **(pear, pair)** of shoes **(affected, effected)** by the heavy rain?

c) I wonder how this will **(affect, effect)** Mary.

512

Review (XII)

a) slighter

b) solemnly

c) thumbs

d) nestled

a) The word in which the **c** has the sound **sh** is:

  decency   precious   acidity   decisive

b) The word in which the **c** has the sound **s** is:

  cautious   talcum   recorded   mincing

c) Who **(rested, wrested)** the throne from King James?

570

bur-den

splen-did

in-vent

Syllables

de-mand-ing re-place-ment (Prefixes and suffixes are separate syllables)

Divide the words below into syllables, following the rule that prefixes and suffixes are separate syllables.

improving settlement deface completely

44

---

a) misspelled

b) rewrite

c) overrun

The only time you may have trouble with the spelling of words to which prefixes have been added is when you find yourself faced by a double letter. Fear it not! Just remember that a prefix does not change the spelling of the original word.

Thus, there are two **s**'s in **misspelled,** two **s**'s in **dissatisfied.** Also there are two **e**'s (with hyphen between) in **re-enter** and two **o**'s in **co-operate.**

103

V. THE PROBLEM OF THE FINAL Y

FINAL Y FOLLOWING A VOWEL

enjoy—enjoys—enjoyed—enjoying

Rule: When the last two letters of a word are a vowel followed by **y, keep** the y when adding any ending.

162

---

a) successive

b) antecedent

c) recession

The "Seed" Words

a) Is a large number of absences **exceesive** or **excessive?**

b) When you concede, are you making a **concession** or a **conceesion?**

c) The Civil War began after one of the colonies had decided upon **(secession, seceesion).**

d) Let us join the **(proceesion, procession).**

221

---

a) sticks

dances

fans

baskets

b) s

c) irregular

NOUNS ENDING IN -S, -CH, -SH, -X, OR -Z

match—matches? wash—washes?

Rule: If a noun ends in **-s, -ch, -sh, -x,** or **-z,** form the plural by adding **-es.**

a) If the plural of **match** is **matches,** then what is the plural of **watch?**

b) What is the plural of each of these words?

walrus march tax topaz

280

Select the correct word:
a) This is a building of unprecedented **(height, hieght)**.

a) heir (no)

b) receive

b) England depends upon her **(foriegn, foreign)** trade.

c) The fishermen were happy when the gang of poachers was **(siezed, seized)**.

d) I've had enough of your **(mischief, mischeif)**. **339**

The Silent B
clamb-er or clam-ber?

a) no

b) no

Remember that the combination **mb** has the sound of **m** when the letters are in the same syllable. The correct division of words into syllables will help you determine when the **mb** is in the same syllable. Our rule has been that we divide between two consonants. Thus, it is **(clamb-er, clam-ber)**. **397**

Homonyms
Select the correct spelling:
a) My wife is **(always, all ways)** happy.

b) I **(always, all ways)** make use of **(all ways, always)** of cutting wood in my mill.

455

---

desert and dessert

a) effect

b) pair

affected

c) affect

Desert is a verb meaning "to leave alone or abandon." A **dessert** is a sweet or pudding ending a meal. (**Desert** as a noun meaning "wasteland" is pronounced with the accent on the first syllable.)
a) He will **(desert, dessert)** when we reach the mountains.

b) She prepared a custard for **(desert, dessert)**. **513**

Review (XII)

a) precious

b) mincing

c) wrested

Select the correct word:
a) Where does the club hold **(it's, its)** meetings?

b) Bach wrote many fine **(choral, coral)** works.

c) Please tell the section chief **(who's, whose)** coming in.

d) The refrigerator is a useful **(applyance, appliance)**. **571**

im-prov-ing

set-tle-ment

de-face

com-plete-ly

Syllables

a) **disappear:** What is the prefix?

b) **replacement:** What is the suffix?

c) **permit:** Divide into two syllables.

d) **applying:** Divide into three syllables.

45

REVIEW (III)

Here is a quick check that combines prefixes with some of the suffixes you have learned. There are three words in dark type incorrectly spelled in the sentence below. Find them and spell them correctly. The **ilegible** letter, **discolored** by rain, was **imovably** stuck on an **impossably** high ledge.

104

Final Y Following a Vowel

Enjoy ends in the vowel **o** followed by the letter **y**. The **y** is **kept** when making other forms of the word **enjoy**. The correct forms are thus (**enjoys, enjoies**) and (**enjoyed, enjoied**).

163

a) excessive

b) concession

c) secession

d) procession

The "Seed" Words

Which sentence contains an error?

a) The lovable old man succeded in being happy.

b) It was admirable of him to exceed his allowance in order to make that gift to the church.

c) It is demonstrable that he acceded to this plan long before he was removed from office.

222

a) watches

b) walruses

marches

taxes

topazes

Regular Noun Plurals and Those Ending in -S, -CH, -SH, -X, or -Z

Select the correct word:

a) The plural of **stork** is (**storks, storkes**).

b) The singular of **hatches** is (**hatch, hatche**).

c) The singular of **lances** is (**lanc, lance**).

d) Write the plural form of the word **box**.

e) The plural of **dozen** is (**dozens, dozenes**).

281

When I Precedes E

a) height

Select the correct word:

b) foreign

a) **mischeivous   mischievous   mischiefous**

c) seized

b) **handkerchiefs   handkercheifs   handkerchieves**

c) **casheired   cashierred   cashiered**

d) mischief

d) **hygeinic   hygienic   hygieneic**

e) **liesurely   leisurely   leisurly**

340

The Silent B

Since the division was **clam-ber,** the **b** is sounded.

clam-ber

Let's apply the same rule to some other words.

a) The correct division is **(thimb-le, thim-ble).**

b) The correct division is **(bomb-ing, bom-bing).**

c) All that he could do was to **(grumb-le, grum-ble).**

398

---

buy, by, and **bye**

a) I want to **buy** a watch.

a) always

b) She works **by** the hour.

c) He received a **bye** when his opponent did not

b) always

appear.

all ways

Use **buy** when you refer to a purchase. Use **by** as a preposition. Use **bye** as a term in sports; its precise meaning varies with the sport.

456

Homonyms

assent and **ascent**

a) desert

The word **assent** means to "agree." **Ascent** is a

b) dessert

noun which designates rising or going higher, and also refers to the slope up which one moves in the process of **ascending.**

514

---

a) its

Review (XII)

b) choral

Select the correct word:

a) When will our fear of war **(cease, sease)?**

c) who's

b) I believe in **(obaying, obeying)** the rules.

c) How many **(oxes, oxen)** are needed for this task?

d) appliance

d) These men are **(Siamese, Siameses).**

572

100

Syllables

a) **dis**appear

b) replace**ment**

c) per-mit

d) ap-ply-ing

It is easier to spell a syllable than it is to spell a word. You are now learning how to divide words into syllables.

fill-ing   rest-ing   in-vent-ing   spell-ing

A **syllable rule:** When a word ends with two consonants, and you are **adding** a suffix, the suffix itself is a separate syllable.

46

Review (III)

illegible

immovably

impossibly

a) The prefix **pre-** plus the root **empt** makes the word ....

b) Correct the spelling of the word **unmistakible,** which uses the root word **mistake.**

c) Combine the word **emphasize** and the prefix **de-.** The new word is ....

105

---

enjoys

enjoyed

a) Which is correct, **stays, stais,** or **stas?**

b) The past form of **stay** is **staied, stayed** or **staed?**

c) Everyone who can **stay** is **(staing, staying, staeing).**

d) The rule to follow in finding the correct answer to a), b) and c) above is that you do not change the last letter of a word that ends in a vowel followed by a......

164

---

a) succeeded

Which two words are misspelled?

a) He defeated three despicable opponents successively.

b) I proceeded to make the necessary arrangments.

c) It would be laughable to intersede in this matter.

d) It is unimaginable that you would supersede me, sir.

223

AN EXCEPTION

a) storks

b) hatch

c) lance

d) boxes

e) dozens

There are exceptions to most of the rules of English spelling. The exceptions are more common when we are dealing with words which have been introduced from foreign languages. In the case of the word **fez,** the tapering felt hat formerly worn by Turkish men, the plural is formed by doubling the final **z,** making the correct spelling **(fezes, fezzes).**

282

a) mischievous
b) handkerchiefs
c) cashiered
d) hygienic
e) leisurely

When I Precedes E
    friend   science   fiery   view
Exceptions to the ei rule:
  a) Use **ie** in the four words at the top of this frame.
  b) Use **ie** with the suffixes **ient** and **ience** whose sounds are **shent** and **shence.**

341

The Silent B
Select the correct answer:

a) thim-ble

b) bomb-ing

c) grum-ble

a) In which of the words below is the **b** silent?
    thumb   **tomboy**   **gamble**   **tumble**
b) In which of these words is the **b** sounded?
    climber   **comb**   **thumbing**   **rumbling**
c) After what letter in the same syllable is the **b** silent?

399

Homonyms
Select the correct word:
a) The sportsman is sometimes a **(buyer, byer)** of rifles.
b) The champion was given a **(by, bye, buy)** in the first round of the tournament.
c) He saw her standing **(by, bye, buy)** the window.

457

Homonyms
    assent and **ascent**
a) Will you **(assent, ascent)** to my trying to make the **(assent, ascent)** of this mountain?
b) His **(assent, ascent)** to the presidency was expected.
c) The guide **(ascented, assented)** to the proposal to climb the mountain after dark.

515

Review (XII)

a) cease

b) obeying

c) oxen

d) Siamese

Select the correct word:
a) The sound of the first **c** in **flaccid** is **(silent, s, k).**
b) The plural of **leaf** is **(leafs, leaves).**
c) Respect the memory of your **(ansestors, ancestors).**
d) The sound of the second **t** in **trestle** is **(heard, silent).**

573

102

Syllables

fill-ing   rest-ing   in-vent-ing   spell-ing

When a word ends with two consonants (such as **fill** or **spell**) then the two consonants remain as part of the same syllable when **-ing** or any other suffix is added.

47

---

a) pre-empt

b) unmistakable

c) de-emphasize

Review (III)

a) Is it **dissolve** or **disolve,** when the root word is **solve?**

b) Is it **mishapen** or **misshapen** when the root word is **shape?**

c) Is it **unnatural** or **unatural** when the root word is **natural?**

106

---

a) stays

b) stayed

c) staying

d) y

Final Y Following a Vowel

a) The word **obey** ends in a vowel followed by a **y.** Other forms of the word should therefore keep the final letter ....

b) I **obey** the same laws that John **(obeis, obeys).**

c) The nobleman issued his orders, and the peasants unfailingly groaned and then **(obeyed, obeied).**

165

---

b) arrangements

c) intercede

Remember: Write your answers on a separate sheet of paper.

DO NOT WRITE IN THIS BOOK.

224

---

fezzes

Select the correct word:

a) The singular of **taxes** is **(tax, taxe).**

b) People who try to vote twice are called **(repeaters, repeateres).**

c) **(Ketchs, ketches)** are sailing vessels which are **(riged, rigged)** fore and aft.

d) The singular of **blazes** is **(blaz, blaze).**

283

Words with the **shent** sound use **ie.**
Select the correct word:
a) The doctor was happy to see the new **(patient, pateint).**
b) Old men were once referred to as **(anceints, ancients).**
c) The parson said that two pounds would be more than **(sufficient, sufficeint).**

342

---

a) thumb

b) rumbling

c) m

The Silent B
Select the correct answer:
a) Which of these words has no **b** sound?
  dumbbell   slumber   dumbest   tremble
b) A sign is a **(symbol, cymbol).**
c) Can you hear the **b** in the word **fumble?**

400

Homonyms

a) buyer

b) bye

c) by

dear and **deer**
Just remember that the name of the animal has two **e**'s. The word **dear** is either a term of affection or a measure of value.
Which are you planning to **(bye, buy)**, the inexpensive tie or the **(deerer, dearer)** one?

458

---

a) assent

  ascent

b) ascent

c) assented

bough and **bow**
A **bough** is a branch of a plant or tree; the verb **bow** means "to bend" and "to curtsy."
a) Did you see how the **(bows, boughs)** of the apple tree **(boughed, bowed)** under the weight of the fruit?
b) Even the trees seemed to **(bow, bough)** to Sir Galahad.

516

---

a) k

b) leaves

c) ancestors

d) silent

Select the correct word:
a) Her performance was amazingly **(compeling, compelling).**
b) The angry fellow was finally **(disuaded, dissuaded).**
c) Some spellings are **(iregular, irregular).**
d) The final step in the plan had been **(omitted, omited).**

574

104

Syllables

The suffix is a separate syllable.

a) What is the last syllable of each word?

catching chilling insisting

b) What is the first syllable of each word?

jumping jumper jumped

48

---

a) dissolve

b) misshapen

c) unnatural

Review (III)

a) The prefix **con-** (meaning with) plus the root **nect** (meaning to fasten) gives the word....................

b) The prefix **inter-** means **between** or **among**. Adding it to the word **related** gives the word ....

107

---

a) y

b) obeys

c) obeyed

Final Y Following a Vowel

a) Honest men obey the laws, and expect no special recognition for **(obeing, obeying).**

b) Every debt is properly **(payible, payable, paiable).**

c) The housekeeper has mislaid her **(kes, keys, keis).**

166

REVIEW (VI)

Select the correct word:

a) At last the ropes were **(untyed, untied).**

b) I was shocked to hear he was **(dieing, dying).**

c) Why is that man **(eyeing, eying)** us so?

d) The contestants are **(vieing, vying)** for a prize.

225

---

a) tax

b) repeaters

c) ketches

 rigged

d) blaze

PLURALS OF NOUNS ENDING IN Y

flys or flies?

Rule: When a noun ends in a y preceded by a consonant, **change the y to an i** before adding **-es** to make the noun plural.

284

When I Precedes E

a) patient

b) ancients

c) sufficient

Select the correct word:

a) The answer in division is the **(quoteint, quotient)**.

b) I find the cash balance **(deficient, deficeint)**.

c) He was admired for his great **(efficeincy, efficiency)**.

d) The new violinist proved himself **(proficient, proficeint)**.

343

The Silent B

a) dumbest

b) symbol

c) yes

Which of the following sentences contain a word with a silent **b**?

a) The king was placed in this ornate tomb.

b) Perhaps we do need a special slumber school.

c) Hillary is one of the world's great climbers.

d) His potential is as yet unplumbed.

401

Homonyms

buy

dearer

dear and deer

a) The deer hold their young very **(deer, dear)**.

b) She **(endeered, endeared)** herself to all.

c) The little deer was his **(deerest, dearest)** friend.

d) Animals love **(endeerments, endearments)**.

459

Homonyms

a) boughs

bowed

b) bow

bridle and bridal

A **bridle** is a special harness for the head of a horse or other animal.

The word **bridal** refers to a bride or to her wedding.

Bridle as a verb means "to resent" or "to restrain."

517

Review (XII)

a) compelling

b) dissuaded

c) irregular

d) omitted

Select the correct word:

a) We find your conclusions **(doutful, doubtful)**.

b) Your interfering is **(recented, resented)**.

c) The garrison continued **(unrelieved, unreleived)**.

d) Close the bottle with this **(stoper, stopper)**.

575

Syllables

Which word in each group of words is correctly divided into syllables? Remember, a suffix is a separate syllable.

a) **jum-ping**   **twis-ter**   **catch-er**   **tas-ted**
b) **tes-ted**   **part-ing**   **hor-ned**   **pac-ker**
c) **form-al**   **col-der**   **farm-er**   **di-ges-ted**

49

IV. THE PROBLEM OF THE FINAL E

The most common errors in spelling occur in words ending with a final silent **e,** to which a suffix is then added. Suffixes, unlike prefixes, often change the spelling of the root words to which they are added. Remember **admirable?** It comes from the word **admire.**

108

Final Y Following a Vowel

a) Who can settle this **(incredable, incredible)** **(arguement, argument)** among the **(boies, boys, bois)?**
b) He was happiest while **(plaing, playing)** games during the weeks that he **(staid, stayed)** at the camp.

167

Review (VI)

Select the correct word:
a) There is no doubt that he **(obeid, obeyed)** the laws.
b) He was calm as he **(testified, testifyed).**
c) Am I ready? You will be surprised at the extent of my **(readyness, readiness).**

226

Nouns Ending in Y

flys or **flies?**

The word **fly** ends in a consonant followed by a **y.** The **y** thus becomes an **i** before **-es** is added to make the noun plural.

The correct spelling thus becomes **(flys, flies).**

285

When I Precedes E

a) quotient

b) deficient

c) efficiency

d) proficient

Select the correct word:

a) The force of ten men was **(insufficeint, insufficient).**

b) The hunter waited with quiet **(patience, pateince).**

c) I have never been so grossly **(decieved, deceived).**

d) This mad tale is quite **(unbelievable, unbeleivable).**

344

The Silent B

Which of these sentences contain words in which the **b** is sounded?

a) tomb

c) climbers

d) unplumbed

a) Why were the rulers **entombed** in pyramids?

b) They were placed in **chambers** with secret entrances.

c) Most of them were **embalmed** at secret rites.

d) These rites **resembled** those of the desert people.

402

Homonyms

a) dear

b) endeared

c) dearest

d) endearments

hear and **here**

The part of your body with which you **hear** is the **ear.** The word describing location is **here.**

a) Have you **(herd, heard)** the latest news?

b) Such impudence is **(unheard, unherd)** of.

c) Everyone is **(here, hear)** at this noisy meeting.

460

Homonyms

bridle and **bridal**

a) He **(bridaled, bridled)** at my rash suggestion.

b) The horse pulling the **(bridle, bridal)** coach wore a new **(bridle, bridal).**

c) I cannot understand the reason for the **(unbridled, unbridaled)** anger displayed by the young groom.

518

Review (XII)

a) doubtful

b) resented

c) unrelieved

d) stopper

Select the correct word:

a) In no case was the **(dosage, doseage)** proper.

b) These **(insuficient, insufficient)** doses did not cure.

c) The doctors found this **(deplorable, deplorible).**

d) Then an **(extrordinary, extraordinary)** thing happened.

576

Syllables

Select the correct way to divide each word into syllables:

a) catch-er

a) **splendid** becomes **splend-id** or **splen-did?**

b) part-ing

b) **abundantly** becomes **a-bun-dan-tly** or **a-bun-dant-ly?**

c) farm-er

c) **darker** becomes **dark-er** or **dar-ker?**

d) **departing** becomes **de-par-ting** or **de-part-ing?** **50**

BEFORE A SUFFIX STARTING WITH A VOWEL

Rule: When a word ends in a silent **e,** drop the final **e** before adding a suffix beginning with a vowel.

If the suffix is **-er,** and the word is **take,** then a person who takes is a **109**

Final Y Following a Vowel

a) incredible
argument
boys

Correct the **incorrect** word in each group:

a) **playing   played   unplayable   replaed**

b) playing
stayed

b) **toys   toyd   toying   toy**

c) **assaying   assayed   assais   assayers**

d) **employer   emploiable   employing   employment**

e) **fray   unfrayed   fraing   frays** **168**

Review (VI)

a) obeyed

Which two sentences contain errors?

b) testified

a) They said he played instead of working.

b) I layed aside my book and began to cry.

c) readiness

c) He said it so shyly that I could not argue.

d) The wine's driness was a welcome surprise.

227

Nouns Ending in Y

allys or **allies?**

a) The word **ally** ends in a **y.** The **y** is preceded by a consonant. The correct plural spelling is **(allys, allies).**

flies

b) The word **lady** also follows our rule, and its plural form becomes **(ladys, ladies).**

c) Which is correct, **countrys** or **countries?** **286**

When I Precedes E

a) insufficient

b) patience

c) deceived

d) unbelievable

Select the correct word:
a) The voice is that of a **(foreigner, foriegner)**.
b) Elizabeth II is the **(riegning, reigning)** monarch of England.
c) A president **(neither, niether)** legislates nor reigns.
d) His actions were those of a true **(freind, friend)**.

345

The Silent B

b) chambers

c) embalmed

d) resembled

Do you hear the **b** in **debt?**
The combination **bt in the same syllable** is similar to the **mb** combination. The **b** is silent. Thus, the **b** is silent in **debt.**
a) Can you hear the **b** in **doubt?**
b) Can you hear the **b** in **indebted?**

403

---

hoarse and horse

a) heard

b) unheard

c) here

The word **horse** refers to the animal. The word **hoarse** refers to a condition of the voice.
a) The rider was quickly **(unhorsed, unhoarsed)**.
b) The Greeks made a hollow wooden **(horse, hoarse)**.
c) His words were marred by his **(horseness, hoarseness)**.

461

Homonyms

a) bridled

b) bridal

bridle

c) unbridled

capital and capitol

Capital refers to a city which is the seat of a government. **Capitol** refers only to the building which is the official seat of government, a statehouse. **Capital** also refers to money or its equivalent. **Capital** also means "major" or "chief" as in capital letters and capital punishment.

519

Review (XII)

a) dosage

b) insufficient

c) deplorable

d) extraordinary

Select the correct word:
a) The disease had suddenly run its **(course, coarse)**.
b) Have you **(proceded, proceeded)** with your work?
c) I **(pleeded, pleaded)** with you to take a rest.
d) Nevertheless, you show this **(insistance, insistence)** on **(continueing, continuing)** your efforts.

577

Suffixes

a) splen-did

b) a-bun-dant-ly

c) dark-er

d) de-part-ing

servant—one who serves; **tourist**—one who tours. There are several suffixes which mean "one who does something." These suffixes are added to other words or word roots. In each case, the new word then has the special meaning—**one who does** whatever the word or root indicates.

51

Before a Suffix Starting with a Vowel

taker

take plus **-er** becomes **taker**

What are some of the suffixes that begin with a vowel? Here are the more common ones:

-er -est -ed -ing -able -ible -y

To the word **take** add the two suffixes from the group above that can best be used with it.

110

Final Y Following a Vowel

a) replayed

b) toyed

c) assays

d) employable

e) fraying

a) The word **employ** follows our rule, for it ends in a vowel followed by **y**. The correct form is therefore **(emploied, employed)**.

b) The **(trolleys, trolleis)** did not run for **(dais, days)**.

c) He is made happy by the **(joys, jois)** of painting.

d) He **(obeis, obeys)** orders without **(saying, saing)** anything.

169

Review (VI)

b) laid

d) dryness

Which three words in the list below are correctly spelled?

conceed	**proceed**	**seceed**
exceed	**preceed**	**succeed**
acceed	**superceed**	**anteceed**
receed	**interceed**	**ceed**

228

Nouns Ending in Y

a) allies

b) ladies

c) countries

Select the correct word:

a) Doctors understand why **(babys, babies)** cry.

b) I cannot believe your **(storys, stories)**.

c) Do you enjoy going to **(parties, partys)**?

d) Broadway is famous for its fine **(plays, plaies)**.

e) The child is happy when playing with the **(toys, toies)**.

287

When I Precedes E

a) foreigner

b) reigning

c) neither

d) friend

Select the correct word:
a) Physics has become a mathematical **(science, sceince)**.
b) The interior of the volcano was a **(feiry, fiery)** oven.
c) I can well appreciate your **(veiwpoint, viewpoint)**.
d) The correct spelling is **(review, reveiw)**.

346

The Silent B

a) no

b) no

Here is a list of sixteen words. Write the six words in which the **b** sound is **not** heard.

slumbering	**amble**	**embalming**	**doubtful**
jumbo	**symbolic**	**bomber**	**trembling**
humbler	**indebted**	**tambourine**	**climbing**
thumbing	**obtain**	**tombs**	**resembled**

404

Homonyms

a) unhorsed

b) horse

c) hoarseness

hour and **our**

The word **hour** refers to the unit of time. **Our** is used to indicate possession.
a) The workers take an **(hourly, ourly) (brake, break)**.
b) We knew by the mark on the case that the clock was **(hours, ours)**.

462

Homonyms

Select the correct word:
a) London is the **(capital, capitol)** of Great Britain.
b) How much **(capital, capitol)** has been invested?
c) Please take me to the **(capital, capitol)** buildings.
d) I do not believe in **(capital, capitol)** punishment.

520

Review (XII)

a) course

b) proceeded

c) pleaded

d) insistence

continuing

Select the correct word:
a) Will you never be **(threw, through)**?
b) Remember not to tear the **(cellophane, celophane)**.
c) His story is an **(exaggeration, exageration)**.
d) Jefferson was a man of high **(principal, principle)**.

578

Suffixes

-ant, -ist, -er, -or

These are the most common suffixes meaning "one who. . . ." Use them to build the word that fulfills each definition.

a) One who assists is called an ....

b) The root **"dent"** means "teeth." One who treats teeth is called a ....

52

---

taker

taking

Do you drop the final **e?**

a) I adore him; in fact, I find him **(adorable, adoreable).**

b) He refused to help me with my **(bakeing, baking).**

c) I approve of your choice, but don't expect my **(approval, approveal)** of everything you do.

d) I was unable to move, even though Jane was **(moveing, moving)** away.

111

---

a) employed

b) trolleys

   days

c) joys

d) obeys

   saying

FINAL Y FOLLOWING A CONSONANT

busy—business   beauty—beautiful

Rule: When the last two letters of a word are a consonant and the letter y, and you add any ending **except** one beginning with an **i:**

Change the final "y" to "i."

170

---

exceed

proceed

succeed

Review (VI)

Select the correct word:

a) He had managed to **(reseed, receed)** the lawn.

b) I **(consede, concede)** that you are correct.

c) Is that the method for **(succeding, succeeding)?**

d) The government's orders **(superseded, super-ceded)** those of the chief constable.

229

---

a) babics

b) stories

c) parties

d) plays

e) toys

Nouns Ending in Y

Were you trapped by **plays** and **toys** in the previous frame? Remember, the change of the final y to i occurs only when the final y is preceded by a consonant!

a) The correct plural of **ray** is **(rayes, rays, raies).**

b) The correct plural of **stay** is **(stayes, stays, staies).**

c) The correct plural of **sty** is **(stys, styes, sties).**

288

113

a) science

b) fiery

c) viewpoint

d) review

Select the correctly spelled word in each group:
a) **inconcievable   inconceiveable   inconceivable**
b) **neighborlyness   neighborliness   nieghborliness**
c) **efficeintly   inefficiently   inefficeintly**
d) **fiercest   feircest   fierceest**
e) **recieptable   receiptible   receiptable**

347

THE SILENT N

thumbing
indebted
bomber
tombs
doubtful
climbing

Can you hear the **n** in **hymn**?
Rule: A final **n** is silent after **m**, when the **mn** combination is in the same syllable and when the **n** is the last letter of the word.
The word **hymn** follows this rule. The **mn** is in the same syllable, and the **n** is the last letter of the word.

405

Homonyms
knew and **new**

a) hourly

break

b) ours

Knew is the past form of the verb **know**. Something which has not previously been used, or appears for the first time, is **new.**
a) They know that I (**new, knew**) who had given them the (**knew, new**) set of dishes.
b) I (**knew, new**) the (**knews, news**) would be good.

463

a) capital

b) capital

c) capitol

d) capital

Homonyms

cite, sight and **site**

Cite means "to quote," or "to name." A **sight** is a view or something special which is seen. It is also used as a verb and means "to see." A **site** is a place or location.

521

a) through

b) cellophane

c) exaggeration

d) principle

Review (XII)

Select the correct word:
a) The armies fought (**desperately, desparately**).
b) He (**led, lead**) the loyal (**oposition, opposition**).
c) Which of the ships have you (**sighted, sited**)?
d) You must study spelling to (**sucsede, succeed**).

579

114

Suffixes

-ant, -ist, -er, -or—the "one who" suffixes
What is the word that matches each definition?

a) assistant

b) dentist

a) One who teaches is called a ....
b) One who does work is a ....
c) If you make a deposit in a bank you are a
....
d) If you invent something, you are an................. **53**

Before a Suffix Starting with a Vowel

a) adorable

b) baking

c) approval

d) moving

What happens to the final **e**?

a) I'm full of hope, and **(hopeing, hoping)** is good for the soul.
b) The pudding was nice—the **(nicest, niceest)** I had ever seen at that restaurant.
c) Most of the first-class passengers decided to dine in the main **(dineing, dining)** salon. **112**

Final Y Following a Consonant

busy—business
The word **busy** ends with the consonant **s** followed by the letter **y**. In adding the suffix **-ness**, change the **y** to an **i**. The correct spelling becomes **(busyness, business)**.

171

VII. DOUBLING THE FINAL CONSONANT

a) reseed

b) concede

c) succeeding

d) superseded

WORDS ENDING IN A SINGLE CONSONANT PRECEDED BY A SINGLE VOWEL

stoped or **stopped**?   **stoping** or **stopping**?
Rule: When a word ends in a **single** consonant preceded by a **single** vowel, **double the final consonant** before adding a suffix beginning with a vowel. **230**

a) rays

b) stays

c) sties

Select the correct word:
a) My favorite colors are the **(grays, grayes, graies)**.
b) The workmen unloaded their tools and were soon **(diging, digging)** the **(ditchs, ditches)**.
c) The locksmith is an expert at repairing **(latches, latchs)**.
d) Whatever led these men to become **(Torys, Toryes, Tories)**? **289**

a) inconceivable

b) neighborliness

c) inefficiently

d) fiercest

e) receiptable

Select the sentences which have **no** errors.

a) Your friend weighs more than his height indicates.

b) The conceited actor received the weird message.

c) The committee yielded, and voted a deficeincy bill.

d) The nieghing of horses is under scientific study.

348

The Silent N

Can you hear the **n** in **hymnal**?

The **n** is silent in **hymn** because **mn** are in the same syllable and the **n** is the last letter of the word. In the word **hymnal,** the **mn** combination is not in the same syllable. Nor is the **n** the last letter of the word. The **n** is therefore **(silent, pronounced)**.

406

a) knew

   new

b) knew

   news

Homonyms

none and nun

The word **none** means "not any." The word **nun** refers to a female member of a religious order.

a) The **(none, nun)** will have **(none, nun)** of your help.

b) **(None, nun)** of the girls will become a **(none, nun)**.

464

Homonyms

cite, sight and site

a) Did you **(cite, sight, site)** the rubble on the new building **(cite, sight, site)**?

b) What authority can you **(cite, sight, site)**?

c) I find this book so **(unsightly, uncitely)** that I cannot **(sight, cite)** its value in the accounts.

522

a) desperately

b) led

   opposition

c) sighted

d) succeed

Some Final Advice

This book should be regarded as an introduction to correct spelling. Thousands of words which you may meet in your writing lifetime have not been included here. However, you have been introduced to the essentials of English spelling. If you follow the ideas and rules in this book, you are on the road to spelling mastery.

580

Suffixes

a) teacher

b) worker

c) depositor

d) inventor

-ant, -ist, -er, -or—the "one who" suffixes

a) One who plays is called a ....

b) One who acts is called an ....

c) One who buys is called a ....

d) One who sails is called a ....

e) One who smokes is called a ....

54

Before a Suffix Starting with a Vowel

a) hoping

b) nicest

c) dining

What happens to the final **e?**

a) The **(strikeing, striking)** workers swore that they would show **(persistance, persistence)** in their strike.

b) What **(imaginable, imagineable)** purpose could she have for such an **(unintelligant, unintelligent)** act?

113

Final Y Following a Consonant

business

beauty—beautiful

The word **beauty** ends with the consonant **t** followed by the letter **y.** Our rule therefore applies. We want to add the suffix **-ful.** First we change the **y** to an **i.** The new word is **(beautiful, beautyful).**

172

Single Consonant Preceded by a Single Vowel

stoped or **stopped?**   **stoping** or **stopping?**

The word **stop** ends with a single consonant **-p.** The letter **p** is preceded by the vowel **-o.** We therefore double the **p** before adding a suffix beginning with a vowel. The correct form is **(stoped, stopped).**

The correct spelling is **(stoping, stopping).**

231

---

a) grays

b) digging

   ditches

c) latches

d) Tories

Nouns Ending in Y

The plural **gray-grays** in the preceding frame is a good introduction to our next rule about plurals. **Rule:** When the final **y** is preceded by a vowel, follow the regular rule of adding **s** to the word.

290

a) and *b*)

When I Precedes E
Select the correct word:
a) He polished the marble with **(proficiency, proficeincy)**.
b) They were special passengers on a **(freighter, frieghter)**.
c) He forced the horse to stop when he pulled the **(riens, reins)**.

349

pronounced

The Silent N
Here is a group of nine words with **mn** combinations. Write the three in which the **n** is silent.

condemn	grimness	solemnity
amnesty	indemnify	hymnal
solemn	hymnology	limn

407

a) nun

b) None

nun

Homonyms
piece and **peace**
A **piece** is a part of something. **Peace** is the absence of conflict or war.
a) Although he likes to take things from other children, he is sometimes a **(peaceful, pieceful)** child.
b) The job was done **(peacemeal, piecemeal)**.

465

a) sight

site

b) cite

c) unsightly

cite

Homonyms
do, dew, and **due**
To **do** is to perform an action; **dew** is the moisture from the air; **due** is a past form meaning "owed."
a) He was soaked by the morning **(do, dew, due)**.
b) What will you **(do, dew, due)** when the book is **(do, dew, due)**?

523

Some Final Advice
Learn to use the dictionary as a guide to spelling. Second, take this book down from time to time and go over its review sections. They contain basic practice in spelling the most important words needed by most people.

581

a) player

b) actor

c) buyer

d) sailor

e) smoker

-able and -ible—the "able to" suffixes

The suffixes **-able** and **-ible** are used to show the addition to the root word of the idea of ability, of being able to do something.

A depend**able** person is one on whom you can depend.

The root **dur** means "lasting." A **durable** thing is something which is able to.................... **55**

---

a) striking

   persistence

b) imaginable

   unintelligent

Before a Suffix Starting with a Vowel

What happens to the final **e**?

a) I am going to write to the editor, and perhaps my **(writing, writeing)** will be of **(significance, significence)**.

b) I intend to continue **(refuseing, refusing)** to accept his **(refusal, refuseal)** of my offer. **114**

---

beautiful

Final Y Following a Consonant

a) **Ready** ends in a consonant followed by a **y**. The correct forms are therefore **(readyly, readily)** and **(readiness, readyness)**.

b) Allow the clothes to dry until they have finished **(driing, drying)**.

c) I was convinced of his guilt despite his repeated and **(plausable, plausible)** **(denyal, denial)**. **173**

---

stopped

stopping

Single Consonant Preceded by a Single Vowel

a) If the last two letters of the word are a vowel followed by a consonant, double the consonant before adding a suffix beginning with a **(vowel, consonant)**.

b) The correct spelling of the word made from **bat** is **(bated, batted)**.

c) Another form of **bat** is **(batting, bating)**. **232**

Nouns Ending in Y
Keep the final Y

a) What is the plural of **alley?** Since it ends in a y preceded by a vowel, the correct spelling of its plural is **(allies, alleyes, alleys)**.

b) For the same reason, the plural of **way** must be **(ways, waies)**. **291**

When I Precedes E

a) proficiency

b) freighter

c) reins

Select the correct word:
a) Blood courses through our **(viens, veins)**.
b) He was dressed in **(prcistly, pricstly)** garb.
c) Pontiac was a great Indian **(cheiftain, chieftain)**.
d) The wrestler is a **(heavyweight, heavywieght)**.

350

The Silent N

condemn

solemn

limn

The word **limn** in the last frame is not a common word. It means "to draw or paint, to portray." Even though **limn** is not often used, it is an excellent example of our silent **n** rule.

Note: The addition of **-ed, -ly, -er,** or **-ing** does not change the silent **n** to a sounded **n. Condemned** has a **(silent, sounded) n.**

408

Homonyms

a) peaceful

b) piecemeal

Select the correct word:
a) The unhappy girl could not help feeling **(blue, blew)**.
b) Every railroad needs its **(brakemen, breakmen)**.
c) Tell me why he spoke so **(horsely, hoarsely)**.

466

Homonyms

a) dew

b) do

due

heel and **heal**

The **heel** is the back of the foot; to **heal** is to cure.
a) What evidence can you **(cite, site)** to prove that this treatment can **(heel, heal)** his wounded **(heel, heal)**?
b) This ointment has a **(healing, heeling) (affect, effect)**.

524

Remember, you **(mispell, misspell)** only through a lack of knowledge and practice!

582

-able, -ible—the "able to" suffixes
a) A visible thing is something you are able to
....
last
b) Something which can be predicted is...............
c) An excitable person is one who can become
....
d) A movable piece of furniture can easily be.........
e) A believable tale is one you are able to............ **56**

---

a) writing

significance

b) refusing

refusal

a) How pure this honey is! It is the **(pureest, purest)** honey **(possible, possable)**.
b) The angry judge was a **(noteable, notable)** fighter.
c) The telephone rang; it was Sue **(telephoneing, telephoning)** to tell us that she was **(coming, comeing)** home as soon as her **(rideing, riding)** lesson was over.

115

---

a) readily

readiness

b) drying

c) plausible

denial

Final Y Following a Consonant
Did you make a mistake in b) of Frame 173?
Driing is incorrect because it would give you a word with a double **i**. Read the rule again, and note that it doesn't apply to endings beginning with **i**. Double i's are very rare in correct English spelling. Keep the final **y**, and the correct spelling is **drying**.

174

Doubling the Final Consonant
Select the correct word:
a) vowel
a) The child **(beged, begged)** for another chance.
b) batted
b) Ulysses was a fine **(runer, runner)**.
c) Whatever are you **(planning, planing)** to do tonight?
c) batting
d) It will do the glass no good to be **(dropped, droped)**.

233

Select the correct word:
a) The addition of alloying elements to steel has resulted in a number of important **(alloyes, alloys)**.
a) alleys
b) Give the biscuits to the **(boys, boies)**.
b) ways
c) The British soldiers were known as **("Tommys," "Tommies")**.
d) What have you done with my **(keys, keyes)**?

292

121

a) veins

b) priestly

c) chieftain

d) heavyweight

When I Precedes E
Select the correct word:
a) They say that the money is (thiers, theirs).
b) The player successfully (fielded, feilded) the ball.
c) He would not (diegn, deign) to consider the offer.

351

silent

Which of these sentences contain words in which there is a sounded **n?**
a) They will go if you **condemn** William.
b) His was the last of the **condemnatory** voices.
c) They walked out of the room **solemnly.**
d) From the music of Bach came many beautiful **hymns.**
e) He paid a heavy **indemnity** for his crime.

409

a) blue

b) brakemen

c) hoarsely

Homonyms
some and **sum**
A **sum** is a total in addition; the word **some** is an inexact measure indicating "a few but not all."
a) We do addition (sumtimes, sometimes).
b) (Some, Sum) of the boys are doing their (somes, sums).
c) Happiness is the (sum, some) of many good deeds.

467

a) cite

heal

heel

b) healing

effect

Homonyms
lesson and **lessen**
A **lesson** is a part of a learning process. To **lessen** something is to cause it to grow smaller or less significant.
a) Have you learned your (lesson, lessen)?
b) How can we (lesson, lessen) the effects of this war?

525

misspell

Now that you have concluded the frames, turn to the last page of the book and again take the test you took on page 9 to see how much you have improved.

583

a) see

b) predictable

c) excited

d) moved

e) believe

You should make a perfect score on all review sections. If not, return to the appropriate frames, and go through them again.

a) What is the prefix in **disappear**?
b) What is the suffix of **eating**?
c) What is the root word of **portable**?
d) What is the middle syllable of **inventing**?   **57**

---

a) purest
   possible
b) notable
c) telephoning
   coming
   riding

Before a Suffix Starting with a Vowel

Select the correctly spelled word in each group:

a) **imovable**   **immoveable**   **immovable**
b) **misstaken**   **mistaken**   **mistakeen**
c) **lovable**   **loveable**   **lovible**

116

---

a) Did you hear the angry (**cryes, cries**) of the crowd?
b) Whatever has happened to the (**babys, babyes, babies**)?
c) I am overjoyed at the news of your (**happiness, happyness**).
d) He was busy until today at his (**busyness, business**).

175

---

a) begged

b) runner

c) planning

d) dropped

Doubling the Final Consonant

Select the correct word:

a) He placed a bet on the (**wining, winning**) horse.
b) The children were (**bussily, busily**) (**digging, diging**) for clams on the windy beach.
c) To their amazement, they found a (**hiden, hidden**) treasure just at the water line.

234

---

a) alloys

b) boys

c) "Tommies"

d) keys

Nouns Ending in Y

Correct the **misspelled** word in each group.

a) **trays   pennies   fillyes   tallies**
b) **cries   sallies   billies   pattys**
c) **kitties ladies   ponies   Mondayes**
d) **monkies queries ferries buoys**
e) **sprays   nayes   parleys   strays**

293

When I Precedes E

Correct the four misspelled words:

sleighing	freindly	weirdly
inveighing	peices	foriegn
siezing	received	cashiers
ceiling	neither	patiently
efficient	fierceness	eighty

352

The Silent N

Which word in each group contains a silent **n**?

a) **damnable damned damnatory damnation**
b) **solemnly solemnified solemnized solemnity**
c) **glumness slimness dimness limned**

410

strait and straight

Something which is not curved to any marked degree is **straight**. A **strait** is either a restriction, a difficulty, or a narrow passage such as that through which water flows between two bodies of land.

a) The weakened ship was in dangerous (**straits, straights**).
b) The Nile River runs (**strait, straight**).

468

Homonyms
lie and lye

Lie means either to recline, or to tell an untruth.
Lye is a name for a strong alkaline substance.

a) She used (**lie, lye**) to make this strong soap.
b) You (**lie, lye**) when you state that I (**permited, permitted**) the dog to (**lie, lye**) on the new coverlet.

526

II. AVOIDING TROUBLES WITH SUFFIXES

a) dis-

b) -ing

c) port-

d) -vent-

The **-ance** and **-ence** endings are easily confused. You cannot always tell which is correct, for they sound the same. Learning how to spell words which end in either **-ance** or **-ence** is largely a matter of memory. However, there are some ideas that can help you.

58

---

a) immovable

b) mistaken

c) lovable

Before a Suffix Starting with a Vowel

Select the correctly spelled word in each group:
a) **grieveance**   **grievance**   **grievence**
b) **immeasurable**   **immeasureable**   **imeasurable**
c) **refuseal**   **refuzal**   **refusal**

117

---

a) cries

b) babies

c) happiness

d) business

Final Y Following a Consonant

What happens to the final y?
a) Are you **(relying, reliing)** on his offer?
b) How many **(replies, replys)** have you received?
c) What is the reason for this **(defyance, defiance)**?
d) Why has she **(denyed, denied)** the obvious truth?

176

---

a) winning

b) busily
   digging

c) hidden

Doubling the Final Consonant

Select the correct word:
a) I find him a **(lovvable, lovable)** man.
b) We cannot fly in such **(fogy, foggy)** weather.
c) What bag? My **(bagage, baggage)** is in my room.
d) It is the **(biggest, bigest)** ship I have ever seen.

235

---

a) fillies

b) patties

c) Mondays

d) monkeys

e) nays

NOUNS ENDING IN F OR FE
knifes or knives?

A special rule: This is a "sometimes" rule—one which you must apply with caution. To form the plural of nouns ending in **f** or **fe**, change the **f** or **fe** to **v** before adding **es**. Knife is one such word. To make it plural, change the **fe** to a **v** and add **es**. The correct spelling is therefore **(knifes, knives)**.

294

seizing

friendly

pieces

forcign

Select the correct word:
a) Give the flowers to my little (neice, niece).
b) Just send him a (brief, breif) note.
c) I'll telephone after the (interview, interveiw).
d) This school teaches a course called (Hygeine, Hygiene).
e) It is foolish to be (overweight, overwieght).

From here go to next frame on page 12 **353**

---

a) damned

b) solemnly

c) limned

THE SOUNDS OF GH
gh—a double silent letter—sometimes.
The **gh** combination is one of the curiosities of the English language. It can have the sound of **f,** as in **cough.** It can have the sound of hard **g,** as in **ghost.** But most often, the **gh** is silent. When working on the frames that follow this one, consult a dictionary whenever the pronunciation of a word is unclear.

From here go to next frame on page 12 **411**

---

a) straits

b) straight

Homonyms
their, there, and they're
Their is used to show possession. **There** indicates location. The contraction **they're** means "they are"; the apostrophe takes the place of **a.**
a) They have lost (their, they're, there) books.
b) What are you doing (their, there)?
c) This is where (there, they're) swimming.

469
From here go to next frame on page 12

---

a) lye

b) lie

permitted

lie

mail and male
Mail refers to letters or to other items delivered by a postman. It can also refer to armor, usually metal. **Male** refers to things masculine or manly.
a) The knight's armor was made of chain (male, mail).
b) Only (males, mails) need apply for jobs delivering (male, mail).

From here go to next frame on page 12 **527**

Tolerance or tolerence? Think of a related word which uses the same root. In this case the word is **tolerate**. Words made from the same root ("toler") tend to use the same letter to begin suffixes. The letter **a** was used in toler**a**te. It should also be used with other suffixes added to the root "toler." The correct spelling is therefore **(tolerance, tolerence)**?

From here go to next frame on page 11 **59**

---

a) grievance

b) immeasurable

c) refusal

Before a Suffix Starting with a Vowel

a) Remember that the glass jar may break in your hand if you try **(forsing, forceing, forcing)** the lid open.

b) The storm had lasted for many days, and we were most delighted to observe that at last the sun was **(shineing, shining, shinneing)**.

From here go to next frame on page 11 **118**

---

a) relying

b) replies

c) defiance

d) denied

Final Y Following a Consonant

What happens to the final **y**?

a) I am **(copying, copiing)** the design of your dress.

b) I would not give a shilling for such **(copies, copys)**.

c) How can one blame a girl for **(trying, triing)**?

d) The children ran home to tell their **(familys, families)**.

From here go to next frame on page 11 **177**

---

a) lovable

b) foggy

c) baggage

d) biggest

Select the correct word:

a) It is the one on which our cargo was **(shiped, shipped)**.

b) The word **rub** becomes **(rubing, rubbing)**.

c) The children were **(happily, happyly)** noisy as they **(draged, dragged)** the wagon along the road.

d) The highwayman laughed as he **(robed, robbed)** the inn.

From here go to next frame on page 11 **236**

---

knives

Nouns Ending in F or FE
Does the ending F or FE become V?

Here are some other common words which follow the rule. In each case, the **f** becomes a **v** before the plural is made by adding **es**.

calf life wharf self half thief leaf scarf loaf elf wife wolf sheaf shelf

You must memorize these words.

From here go to next frame on page 12 **295**

SPELLING TEST

1.	Plausible	His story was not very **plausible**.	Plausible
2.	Secretary	Have you seen the new **secretary**?	Secretary
3.	Dissatisfied	Why are you so **dissatisfied**?	Dissatisfied
4.	Psychological	The book is a **psychological** study.	Psychological
5.	Misspelled	The word has been **misspelled**.	Misspelled
6.	Principle	Archimedes' **principle** should be mastered.	Principle
7.	Succeed	You will **succeed** if you want to.	Succeed
8.	Secede	The states wanted to **secede**.	Secede
9.	Necessary	It is **necessary** to drive carefully.	Necessary
10.	Principal	The **principal** figure is Holmes.	Principal
11.	Stationery	This store sells candy and **stationery**.	Stationery
12.	Manageable	The horse proved easily **manageable**.	Manageable
13.	Occurrence	The fire was a tragic **occurrence**.	Occurrence
14.	Stationary	My boss's desk is **stationary**.	Stationary
15.	Receivable	The account is now **receivable**.	Receivable
16.	Fluorescent	Most desk lamps are **fluorescent**.	Fluorescent
17.	Exhilaration	I could not explain his **exhilaration**.	Exhilaration
18.	Independent	At last he has become **independent**.	Independent
19.	Superintendent	Is your **superintendent** efficient?	Superintendent
20.	Miscellaneous	He sells **miscellaneous** items at home.	Miscellaneous
21.	Contemptible	It was a **contemptible** action.	Contemptible
22.	Temperament	Many singers are fiery by **temperament**.	Temperament
23.	Accommodate	How many people will the car **accommodate**?	Accommodate
24.	Eighth	Is he **eighth** or ninth in line?	Eighth
25.	Ecstasy	Her happiness was close to **ecstasy**.	Ecstasy